PREFACE

As a 19-year-old and firstborn, I can boldly say I've had my fair share of ups and downs: the feeling of not being enough, not moving, letting loved ones down, pressure from society, striving to please my parents, and extreme anxiety about the near future. It was nothing short of depressing. I thank God, above all, for setting me free and being my backbone through it all. I was one of the painfully ever-increasing number of porn and masturbation addicts, but God set me free and pulled me through, even when I fell a million times. It's often tempting to seek definition and significance in a world that offers a myriad of labels. But when we chase validation in temporary sources, hoping they'll define us, we only find fleeting satisfaction. Our identity is found in Christ when we're anchored in contentment, gratitude, and a deep relationship with God that leads to seeking His kingdom and righteousness. Follow God consistently and committedly all the days of your life... This book is not for the lazy, the ones looking to make it big in 2 weekends, or the ones fascinated by big numbers. It's aimed towards those who would put one foot in front of the other each day until they, maybe slowly, but surely get to their destination. This book has something for everyone. Enjoy!

The book '100 Ways to Make a Million Dollars a Year' is a compilation of strategies and insights aimed at providing educational and informational value to readers seeking financial success. While real-life examples and references may be included for illustrative purposes, all content presented in this book is based on the author's original research, analysis, and expertise. Any resemblance to actual individuals, businesses, or events is coincidental and unintended. The author and publisher have taken measures to ensure the accuracy and reliability of the information provided, but make no guarantees or warranties regarding its completeness or suitability for any specific purpose. Readers are encouraged to verify information independently and consult with qualified professionals before making financial decisions. The author and publisher disclaim any liability for the consequences of actions taken by readers based on the information presented in this book.

Copyrights © 2024 by Titus Bankwell

All rights reserved.

Table of Contents

1. Anesthesiologist...9
2. Start a Successful Tech Startup and Scale It Rapidly 10
3. Invest in High-Growth Stocks or Venture Capital 11
4. Build and Monetize a Popular YouTube Channel 12
5. Develop and Sell a Profitable Mobile App 13
6. Create and Sell Online Courses or Educational Materials 15
7. Become a Successful Real Estate Investor.......15
8. Provide Consulting Services to Corporations or Individuals...16
9. Build a Large Following on Social Media and Monetize It Through Sponsored Posts and Partnerships....................17
10. Write and Publish Bestselling Books or E-books...........19
11. Invest in Rental Properties and Earn Passive Income.....20
12. Develop and License Patented Inventions or Technology..21
13. Trade Cryptocurrencies or Forex Markets Profitably......22
14. Start a Successful E-commerce Store Selling Niche Products..23
15. Offer High-End Coaching or Mentorship Programs......24
16. Create and Sell Digital Products Such as Templates, Designs, or Software Tools..................................26
17. Become a Professional Speaker and Earn Fees for Public Appearances...27
18. Start a Successful Podcast and Monetize It Through Sponsorships and Advertising.................................28
19. Launch a Franchise Business with Multiple Locations....29

20. Invest in Renewable Energy Projects or Green Technology..................31
21. Build and Monetize a Popular Blog Through Affiliate Marketing and Sponsored Content..................32
22. Provide Specialized Medical or Legal Services..................33
23. Develop and Sell a Successful Online Marketplace..........34
24. Offer High-End Luxury Services Such as Personal Concierge or Event Planning..................36
25. Start a Successful Dropshipping Business..................37
26. Invest in Commercial Real Estate Properties..................38
27. Offer High-Ticket Consulting Services to Businesses.....40
28. Develop and Sell a Successful Mobile Game..................41
29. Start a Successful SaaS (Software as a Service) Business..................43
30. Provide High-End Graphic Design or Branding Services..................44
31. Become a Successful Freelance Writer or Copywriter.....45
32. Offer High-End Interior Design or Architectural Services..................47
33. Invest in Precious Metals Such as Gold or Silver............48
34. Start a Successful Affiliate Marketing Business................50
35. Offer Specialized IT or Cybersecurity Consulting Services..................51
36. Develop and Sell a Successful Online Fitness Program..53
37. Provide Specialized Financial Planning or Wealth Management Services..................54
38. Invest in Blue-Chip Stocks with a Proven Track Record..................56
39. Start a Successful Clothing Line or Fashion Brand..........57
40. Offer Specialized Marketing or Advertising Services......59
41. Invest in Art or Collectibles with Potential for Appreciation..................60

42. Develop and Sell a Successful Online Dating Platform..62
43. Offer Specialized Coaching or Training for Athletes or Performers..................63
44. Invest in Dividend-Paying Stocks for Steady Income.....65
45. Start a Successful Food Delivery Service or Meal Prep Business..................66
46. Offer Specialized Language Translation or Interpretation Services..................68
47. Develop and Sell a Successful Mobile Productivity App..................70
48. Invest in Emerging Markets with High Growth Potential..................71
49. Start a Successful Pet Care or Grooming Business..........73
50. Offer Specialized Engineering or Technical Consulting Services..................75
51. Develop and Sell a Successful Online Productivity Tool..................77
52. Invest in Rental Properties in Tourist Destinations..........78
53. Start a Successful Personal Branding Agency..................80
54. Offer Specialized Event Management or Wedding Planning Services..................82
55. Develop and Sell a Successful Online Therapy Platform..................83
56. Invest in Index Funds for Diversified Exposure to the Market..................85
57. Start a Successful Influencer Marketing Agency..............87
58. Offer Specialized HR Consulting or Recruitment Services..................89
59. Develop and Sell a Successful Online Travel Booking Platform..................90
60. Invest in Real Estate Investment Trusts (REITs) for Passive Income..................92

61. Start a Successful Digital Marketing Agency...................94
62. Offer Specialized Executive Coaching or Leadership Development Program..95
63. Develop and Sell a Successful Online Language Learning Platform...97
64. Invest in Peer-to-Peer Lending Platforms for High Returns...99
65. Start a Successful Subscription Box Service....................101
66. Offer Specialized Data Analysis or Business Intelligence Services...103
67. Develop and Sell a Successful Online Cooking or Recipe Platform..104
68. Invest in High-Quality Dividend-Paying Bonds............106
69. Start a Successful Influencer Management Agency........108
70. Offer Specialized HR Consulting or Recruitment Services...109
71. Develop and Sell a Successful Online Music Streaming Platform..111
72. Invest in Angel Investing or Startup Incubators............113
73. Start a Successful Digital Advertising Agency................114
74. Offer Specialized Healthcare Consulting or Telemedicine Services...116
75. Develop and Sell a Successful Online Art Marketplace...118
76. Invest in Rental Properties for Student Housing...........120
77. Start a Successful SEO (Search Engine Optimization) Agency..121
78. Offer Specialized Sustainability Consulting or Green Energy Solutions...123
79. Develop and Sell a Successful Online Tutoring Platform..125

80. Invest in Cryptocurrencies with High Growth Potential...........127
81. Start a Successful Virtual Assistant Staffing Agency......128
82. Offer Specialized Insurance Consulting or Risk Management Services...........130
83. Develop and Sell a Successful Online Craft or DIY Marketplace...........132
84. Invest in Blue-Chip Mutual Funds for Long-Term Growth...........134
85. Start a Successful Content Marketing Agency...........135
86. Offer Specialized Corporate Training or Development Programs...........137
87. Develop and Sell a Successful Online Gardening or Landscaping Platform...........139
88. Invest in High-Quality Real Estate Crowdfunding Projects...........141
89. Start a Successful SEO (Search Engine Optimization) Agency...........142
90. Offer Specialized Sustainability Consulting or Green Energy Solutions...........144
91. Start a Successful Software Development Outsourcing Company...........146
92. Offer Specialized Diversity and Inclusion Consulting Services...........150
93. Develop and Sell a Successful Online Mindfulness or Meditation Platform...........151
94. Invest in High-Quality Art Funds or Collectibles Portfolios...........153
95. Develop and Sell a Successful Online Parenting or Childcare Platform...........153
96. Investing in Yourself through Continuous Learning and Personal Development...........155.

97. Become a Professional Athlete..157
98. Start a Successful Social Media Management Agency...159
99. Offer Specialized Legal Consulting or Compliance Services..161
100. Become a High-Profile Musician.............................163

LET'S GET IT!

Generating a yearly income of one million dollars is attainable through diverse avenues, albeit typically necessitating a blend of proficiency, diligence, and occasional serendipity.

Presented below is an extensive catalog of 100 feasible methods to generate an annual income of one million dollars:

1. **Anesthesiologist:**

Anesthesiologists are highly trained medical professionals responsible for administering anesthesia to patients undergoing surgical procedures. They ensure the safe delivery of anesthesia and monitor patients' vital signs throughout the surgical process.

Case Study:

Dr. Emily Roberts established herself as a successful anesthesiologist by completing her residency at a renowned medical center and later joining a private practice specializing in complex surgical procedures. Through strategic networking and providing exceptional patient care, Dr. Roberts expanded her practice, earning over a million dollars annually.

Getting Started:

- Complete undergraduate studies with a focus on pre-medical courses.
- Attend medical school and obtain a Doctor of Medicine (MD) degree.
- Complete a residency program in anesthesiology, typically lasting 4 years.

- Pursue fellowship training to specialize in areas such as pediatric anesthesia, cardiac anesthesia, or pain management.
- Join a hospital, medical group, or academic institution to practice as a board-certified anesthesiologist, negotiate competitive compensation packages, and explore additional income opportunities through teaching or consulting.

2. **Start a Successful Tech Startup and Scale It Rapidly:**

Starting a tech startup involves identifying a market need, developing innovative solutions using technology, and scaling the business rapidly to achieve significant growth and profitability.

Case Study:

XYZ Tech, founded by James Smith and his team of tech enthusiasts, disrupted the e-commerce industry with its AI-driven recommendation engine. Through strategic partnerships, aggressive marketing campaigns, and continuous product innovation, XYZ Tech achieved exponential growth, securing millions in funding, and generating over a million dollars in annual revenue within two years of launch.

Getting Started:

- Conduct market research to identify underserved markets or pain points that can be addressed through technological innovation.

- Develop a Minimum Viable Product (MVP) to validate the product-market fit and gather feedback from early adopters.
- Secure funding through bootstrapping, angel investors, venture capital firms, or crowdfunding platforms to fuel product development and initial market penetration.
- Build a talented and diverse team of engineers, designers, and marketers to execute the vision and scale the startup efficiently.
- Implement agile methodologies, iterate based on customer feedback, and focus on user acquisition, retention, and monetization strategies to drive rapid growth.

3. Invest in High-Growth Stocks or Venture Capital:

Investing in high-growth stocks or venture capital involves allocating capital to companies or startups with the potential for significant appreciation in value, thereby generating substantial returns on investment.

Case Study:

Sarah Johnson, a savvy investor with a keen eye for disruptive technologies, achieved millionaire status by investing in high-growth stocks like Amazon, Tesla, and Netflix during their early stages. Additionally, Sarah diversified her investment portfolio by participating in successful venture capital rounds for startups such as Airbnb and Uber, reaping substantial returns on her investments.

Getting Started:

- Conduct thorough research on companies, industries, and market trends to identify high-growth investment opportunities.
- Diversify investment portfolios across various asset classes, sectors, and geographic regions to mitigate risk and maximize returns.
- Consider investing in early-stage startups through venture capital funds or angel investing networks to capitalize on potential high returns in exchange for higher risk.
- Stay informed about macroeconomic factors, regulatory changes, and technological advancements that may impact investment decisions.
- Monitor and rebalance investment portfolios regularly to optimize returns and minimize exposure to market volatility.

4. Build and Monetize a Popular YouTube Channel:

Building and monetizing a popular YouTube channel involves creating engaging content, growing a loyal audience, and leveraging various monetization strategies to generate revenue from advertisements, sponsorships, merchandise sales, and memberships.

Case Study:

The Tech Insider, a YouTube channel managed by Alex Johnson, gained immense popularity by providing in-depth reviews, tutorials, and tech-related content. Through strategic collaborations with tech brands, affiliate partnerships, and merchandise sales, The Tech Insider amassed millions of subscribers and generated over a million dollars annually in revenue.

Getting Started:

- Identify a niche or target audience based on your interests, expertise, and market demand.
- Create high-quality and compelling content that resonates with your target audience, incorporating engaging visuals, storytelling, and value-added information.
- Optimize video titles, descriptions, tags, and thumbnails for search engine optimization (SEO) to increase visibility and attract more viewers.
- Monetize your YouTube channel through the YouTube Partner Program, where you can earn revenue from advertisements displayed on your videos, as well as explore additional income streams such as sponsored content, affiliate marketing, merchandise sales, and channel memberships.
- Engage with your audience by responding to comments, collaborating with other creators, hosting live streams or Q&A sessions, and nurturing a sense of community to foster loyalty and encourage repeat viewership.

5. Develop and Sell a Profitable Mobile App:

Developing and selling a profitable mobile app involves identifying a market need, conceptualizing an innovative app idea, designing and developing a user-friendly interface, and monetizing through app sales, in-app purchases, subscriptions, or advertisements.

Case Study:

FitnessPal, a mobile app developed by Jane Smith, gained widespread popularity among health and fitness enthusiasts by offering personalized workout plans, nutrition tracking, and progress monitoring features. Through strategic pricing strategies and premium subscription offerings, FitnessPal generated millions in revenue through app downloads and in-app purchases.

Getting Started:

- Conduct market research to identify gaps or opportunities in the mobile app market, analyze competitor offerings, and understand user preferences and behaviors.
- Define the core features and functionalities of your mobile app, focusing on solving a specific problem or addressing a particular need for your target audience.
- Design an intuitive and visually appealing user interface (UI) and user experience (UX) that enhances usability and engagement.
- Develop the mobile app using the appropriate programming languages, frameworks, and development tools, ensuring compatibility across different devices and operating systems.
- Implement effective monetization strategies such as offering the app as a paid download, integrating in-app purchases or subscriptions for premium content or features, and incorporating advertisements or sponsored content to generate additional revenue.

6. Create and Sell Online Courses or Educational Materials:

Creating and selling online courses or educational materials involves leveraging your expertise, knowledge, and skills to develop valuable learning resources that cater to a specific target audience or niche market.

Case Study:

John Doe, a digital marketing expert, generated over a million dollars in revenue by offering comprehensive online courses on SEO, social media marketing, and email marketing, attracting thousands of students worldwide.

Getting Started:

- Identify your area of expertise, passion, or subject matter knowledge that you can leverage to create valuable educational content for your target audience.
- Research the demand for online courses or educational materials in your chosen niche, analyze competitor offerings, and understand the needs and preferences of your target audience.
- Develop high-quality and comprehensive course content.

7. Become a Successful Real Estate Investor:

Real estate investing involves purchasing properties with the intention of generating income through rental payments, property appreciation, or real estate development.

Case Study:

Mark Johnson built a multi-million dollar real estate portfolio by acquiring residential properties in high-demand rental markets. Through strategic property management, renovation projects, and leveraging financing options, Mark achieved substantial cash flow and property appreciation, earning over a million dollars annually.

Getting Started:

- Educate yourself about real estate investment strategies, market dynamics, and financing options through books, courses, or mentorship programs.
- Identify target markets with strong rental demand, population growth, and economic stability to maximize rental income potential and property appreciation.
- Analyze investment properties based on factors such as location, property condition, rental income potential, and return on investment (ROI).
- Secure financing through mortgages, private lenders, or real estate investment partnerships to acquire investment properties.
- Implement effective property management practices to maintain and enhance property value, minimize vacancies, and maximize rental income.

8. Provide Consulting Services to Corporations or Individuals:

Consulting services involve offering expert advice, guidance, and solutions to corporations or individuals in various industries or domains.

Case Study:

Emily Watson established herself as a sought-after management consultant by leveraging her extensive experience in business strategy and organizational development. Through strategic networking, delivering high-impact consulting projects, and cultivating long-term client relationships, Emily built a successful consulting practice, earning over a million dollars annually.

Getting Started:

- Identify your area of expertise, industry knowledge, or specialized skill set that can add value to clients seeking consulting services.
- Build a professional network and establish credibility through thought leadership, speaking engagements, or publishing industry-related content.
- Define your consulting service offerings, target market segments, and pricing structure based on the value delivered and market demand.
- Market your consulting services through targeted outreach, referrals, and digital marketing channels to attract potential clients.
- Deliver exceptional consulting services, prioritize client satisfaction, and continuously seek feedback to improve service delivery and build a reputation for excellence.

9. **Build a Large Following on Social Media and Monetize It Through Sponsored Posts and Partnerships:**

Building a large following on social media platforms such as Instagram, YouTube, or TikTok enables individuals to leverage their influence and monetize their online presence through sponsored posts, brand partnerships, and affiliate marketing.

Case Study:

Sarah Smith, a lifestyle influencer with millions of followers on Instagram, collaborates with fashion, beauty, and lifestyle brands to create sponsored content and promotional campaigns. Through strategic brand partnerships, sponsored posts, and affiliate marketing, Sarah monetizes her social media following, earning over a million dollars annually.

Getting Started:

- Choose social media platforms aligned with your interests, expertise, or target audience demographics to focus your content creation efforts.
- Create high-quality, engaging content that resonates with your audience, incorporating visual storytelling, authenticity, and value-added information.
- Build and nurture relationships with your followers by actively engaging with comments, responding to messages, and fostering a sense of community.
- Collaborate with brands, businesses, or influencers in your niche through sponsored posts, product endorsements, brand ambassadorships, or affiliate partnerships.
- Diversify revenue streams by exploring additional monetization opportunities such as selling digital products, offering premium content or services, or launching merchandise lines.

10. Write and Publish Bestselling Books or E-books:

Writing and publishing bestselling books or e-books offer authors the opportunity to generate substantial income through book sales, royalties, and ancillary revenue streams such as speaking engagements, coaching programs, or merchandise sales.

Case Study:

John Doe, a prolific author in the personal development genre, achieved millionaire status by writing and publishing multiple bestselling books on topics such as success mindset, productivity, and leadership. Through effective book marketing strategies, building a loyal reader base, and expanding his platform through speaking engagements and media appearances, John generated significant royalties and ancillary income from his book sales.

Getting Started:

- Identify a niche or topic that resonates with your expertise, passion, or target audience interests to guide your book writing efforts.
- Develop a compelling book concept, outline, and manuscript, focusing on providing valuable insights, practical advice, or compelling storytelling.
- Choose a publishing route that aligns with your goals and resources, whether traditional publishing, self-publishing, or hybrid publishing models.
- Implement effective book marketing strategies to promote your book, including online and offline channels such as social media, book signings, media interviews, and book launch events.

- Leverage your book's success to explore additional revenue opportunities such as speaking engagements, coaching programs, online courses, or merchandise sales.

11. Invest in Rental Properties and Earn Passive Income:

Investing in rental properties involves acquiring residential or commercial real estate assets and generating passive income through rental payments from tenants.

Case Study:

Jane Williams achieved financial independence by building a diversified portfolio of rental properties across different geographic locations. Through diligent property selection, proactive property management, and optimizing rental income, Jane generated substantial passive income streams, exceeding a million dollars annually.

Getting Started:

- Conduct thorough market research to identify promising rental property markets with strong demand, rental yield potential, and favorable economic conditions.
- Analyze investment properties based on factors such as location, property condition, rental income potential, financing options, and potential for property appreciation.
- Develop a financing strategy to fund property acquisitions, including options such as traditional mortgages, private financing, or real estate investment partnerships.

- Implement effective property management practices to maintain and enhance property value, minimize vacancies, and maximize rental income.
- Continuously monitor market trends, rental property performance, and regulatory changes to adapt investment strategies and optimize returns.

12. Develop and License Patented Inventions or Technology:

Developing and licensing patented inventions or technology involves creating innovative products, processes, or solutions, securing intellectual property rights through patents, and monetizing them through licensing agreements with third-party companies or organizations.

Case Study:

David Johnson, an inventor and entrepreneur, developed a patented technology for renewable energy generation. By licensing his technology to utility companies and renewable energy firms, David earned substantial royalties and licensing fees, surpassing a million dollars annually.

Getting Started:

- Identify a problem or opportunity that can be addressed through innovative technological solutions, and conduct research to assess the feasibility and market potential.
- Develop prototypes, conduct testing, and refine the invention to demonstrate its efficacy, functionality, and commercial viability.

- File patent applications to protect intellectual property rights, working with patent attorneys or agents to navigate the patenting process and secure granted patents.
- Identify potential licensees or partners who can benefit from the patented technology and negotiate licensing agreements that provide favorable terms and royalties.
- Monitor and enforce patent rights, including licensing compliance, infringement detection, and legal action if necessary, to protect intellectual property and maximize licensing revenue.

13. **Trade Cryptocurrencies or Forex Markets Profitably:**

Trading cryptocurrencies or forex markets involves buying and selling digital currencies or foreign currencies with the goal of profiting from price fluctuations and market trends.

Case Study:

Michael Smith, a skilled trader and investor, achieved significant wealth through successful trading in cryptocurrencies and forex markets. By developing disciplined trading strategies, conducting thorough market analysis, and managing risk effectively, Michael consistently generated substantial returns, exceeding a million dollars annually.

Getting Started:

- Educate yourself about cryptocurrency and forex trading fundamentals, including market dynamics, technical

analysis, and risk management principles, through courses, books, or online resources.
- Open a trading account with a reputable cryptocurrency exchange or forex broker, ensuring compliance with regulatory requirements and security best practices.
- Develop a trading plan that outlines your trading goals, risk tolerance, entry and exit strategies, position sizing, and trade management rules.
- Practice trading with virtual or demo accounts to gain experience, refine your trading strategies, and build confidence before risking real capital.
- Start trading with a small amount of capital, gradually increasing your position sizes as you gain proficiency and achieve consistent profitability.

14. Start a Successful E-commerce Store Selling Niche Products:

Starting a successful e-commerce store involves identifying a niche market or product category, sourcing high-quality products, building an online storefront, and implementing effective marketing and sales strategies to attract customers and drive sales.

Case Study:

Sarah Jones launched an e-commerce store specializing in eco-friendly home goods and sustainable lifestyle products. Through targeted marketing campaigns, strategic partnerships with eco-conscious brands, and exceptional customer service, Sarah's e-commerce store gained traction and generated over a million dollars in annual revenue.

Getting Started:

- Research niche markets or product categories with high demand, low competition, and passionate customer segments, and validate market demand through surveys, keyword research, and competitor analysis.
- Source or manufacture high-quality products that meet the needs and preferences of your target audience, emphasizing unique selling propositions such as product quality, sustainability, or exclusivity.
- Build an e-commerce website or utilize existing platforms such as Shopify, WooCommerce, or Amazon to create a professional online storefront, incorporating user-friendly navigation, compelling product descriptions, and seamless checkout processes.
- Implement digital marketing strategies such as search engine optimization (SEO), social media marketing, email marketing, and influencer partnerships to drive traffic to your e-commerce store and convert visitors into customers.
- Continuously optimize your e-commerce operations, including inventory management, customer support, order fulfillment, and website performance, to maximize sales and customer satisfaction.

15. **Offer High-End Coaching or Mentorship Programs:**

Offering high-end coaching or mentorship programs involves leveraging your expertise, experience, and insights to provide personalized guidance, support, and accountability to clients seeking to achieve specific goals or overcome challenges.

Case Study:

Jessica Williams, a successful business coach and mentor, established a premium coaching program for aspiring entrepreneurs and executives. Through one-on-one coaching sessions, group masterminds, and intensive workshops, Jessica helped her clients unlock their full potential, achieve breakthrough results, and command premium fees, generating over a million dollars annually.

Getting Started:

- Identify your area of expertise, coaching niche, or target audience demographics based on your skills, knowledge, and experience.
- Define your coaching or mentorship program offerings, including program duration, format (e.g., one-on-one coaching, group coaching, online courses), and pricing structure.
- Develop a compelling value proposition and marketing message that highlights the benefits, outcomes, and transformational results your coaching program delivers to clients.
- Build your personal brand and online presence through thought leadership, content creation, speaking engagements, and networking to attract potential clients and establish credibility in your coaching niche.
- Provide exceptional coaching services, personalized support, and tangible results to your clients, fostering trust, loyalty, and referrals, and continuously iterate and

improve your coaching methodologies based on client feedback and outcomes.

16. Create and Sell Digital Products Such as Templates, Designs, or Software Tools:

Creating and selling digital products involves developing valuable digital assets such as templates, designs, software tools, or digital downloads, and monetizing them through online marketplaces, e-commerce platforms, or direct sales.

Case Study:

Alex Johnson, a graphic designer, established a successful online business selling digital design templates and assets. By leveraging platforms such as Etsy, Creative Market, and his own website, Alex reached a global audience of designers and creatives, generating substantial passive income from his digital product sales.

Getting Started:

- Identify a niche or target audience for your digital products, focusing on specific industries, interests, or pain points.
- Create high-quality digital products such as graphic design templates, website themes, software plugins, or educational resources that provide value and solve customer needs.
- Set up an online storefront or leverage existing marketplaces to showcase and sell your digital products, optimizing product listings, descriptions, and imagery to attract buyers.

- Implement digital marketing strategies such as email marketing, content marketing, social media promotion, and search engine optimization (SEO) to drive traffic to your online store and increase sales.
- Continuously iterate and update your digital products based on customer feedback, market trends, and technological advancements to maintain relevance and competitiveness.

17. Become a Professional Speaker and Earn Fees for Public Appearances:

Becoming a professional speaker involves leveraging your expertise, knowledge, or personal story to deliver compelling presentations, keynote speeches, or workshops at conferences, events, and corporate gatherings, and earning fees for your speaking engagements.

Case Study:

Michael Smith, an expert in leadership and motivation, built a successful speaking career by sharing his insights and experiences with audiences worldwide. Through captivating storytelling, engaging delivery, and valuable content, Michael commanded high speaking fees and secured recurring bookings at prestigious events, earning over a million dollars annually.

Getting Started:

- Identify your speaking niche or area of expertise, whether it's leadership, entrepreneurship, personal development, industry-specific topics, or motivational speaking.

- Develop your speaking skills and presentation abilities through practice, training programs, and attending speaking events or workshops.
- Build a professional speaker brand and online presence through a personal website, speaker reels, testimonials, and promotional materials showcasing your expertise and speaking topics.
- Network with event organizers, conference planners, and industry associations to secure speaking opportunities, pitch your speaking services, and negotiate speaking fees and terms.
- Deliver impactful and memorable presentations, tailor your content to the needs and interests of each audience, and consistently deliver value to build your reputation as a sought-after speaker.

18. Start a Successful Podcast and Monetize It Through Sponsorships and Advertising:

Starting a successful podcast involves creating engaging audio content on topics of interest to your target audience, building a loyal listener base, and monetizing your podcast through sponsorships, advertising, listener support, and premium content offerings.

Case Study:

Sarah Johnson, host of "The Entrepreneur's Journey" podcast, achieved financial success by sharing inspiring stories, practical insights, and expert interviews with aspiring and established entrepreneurs. Through strategic partnerships with sponsors, affiliate marketing, and listener donations, Sarah monetized her podcast, generating over a million dollars annually.

Getting Started:

- Identify a niche or topic for your podcast that aligns with your interests, expertise, or target audience demographics, and conduct market research to assess demand and competition.
- Plan your podcast format, content structure, and episode topics, focusing on providing value, entertainment, and actionable insights to your listeners.
- Set up recording equipment, choose a podcast hosting platform, and produce high-quality audio content, incorporating engaging storytelling, interviews, and audience interaction.
- Promote your podcast through social media, email newsletters, guest appearances on other podcasts, and collaborations with influencers to attract listeners and grow your audience.
- Monetize your podcast through sponsorships, advertising, affiliate marketing, listener donations, premium subscriptions, or merchandise sales, leveraging your audience reach and engagement to generate revenue streams.

19. **Launch a Franchise Business with Multiple Locations:**

Launching a franchise business involves replicating a successful business model and brand by offering franchise opportunities to entrepreneurs or investors to operate and manage their own franchise locations under your brand name.

Case Study:

Jane Smith, founder of "Healthy Bites Cafe," expanded her business through franchising, allowing aspiring entrepreneurs to own and operate their own Healthy Bites Cafe locations. By providing comprehensive training, ongoing support, and a proven business model, Jane successfully scaled her franchise business, opening multiple locations and generating significant franchise fees and royalties.

Getting Started:

- Develop a scalable and replicable business model that has demonstrated success and profitability, with clear brand identity, operational processes, and market demand.
- Create a franchise disclosure document (FDD) outlining the franchise opportunity, including franchise fees, royalties, training, support, and other terms and conditions.
- Recruit and qualify potential franchisees through targeted marketing, franchise expos, and networking events, ensuring alignment with your brand values, vision, and financial qualifications.
- Provide comprehensive training and ongoing support to franchisees, including operations, marketing, and business development, to ensure consistency and quality across all franchise locations.
- Continuously monitor and support franchise operations, enforce brand standards and quality control, and facilitate communication and collaboration among franchisees to drive collective success and growth.

20. Invest in Renewable Energy Projects or Green Technology:

Investing in renewable energy projects or green technology involves allocating capital to companies, projects, or initiatives that develop and deploy environmentally sustainable solutions for energy generation, resource conservation, or pollution reduction.

Case Study:

David Johnson, a socially responsible investor, achieved financial success by investing in renewable energy projects such as solar farms, wind turbines, and biomass facilities. By supporting companies at the forefront of green technology innovation, David not only generated attractive financial returns but also contributed to environmental sustainability and positive social impact.

Getting Started:

- Research renewable energy sectors and technologies such as solar, wind, hydroelectric, biomass, geothermal, and energy storage to understand market trends, investment opportunities, and regulatory frameworks.
- Evaluate investment options including publicly traded renewable energy companies, infrastructure funds, project finance opportunities, green bonds, and impact investment funds focusing on environmental sustainability.
- Assess investment risks and returns based on factors such as project economics, technology maturity,

regulatory incentives, environmental impact, and long-term growth prospects.
- Diversify investment portfolios across different renewable energy sectors, geographic regions, and asset classes to mitigate risk and optimize returns.
- Monitor industry developments, policy changes, and technological advancements to identify emerging opportunities and adjust investment strategies accordingly.

21. Build and Monetize a Popular Blog Through Affiliate Marketing and Sponsored Content:

Building and monetizing a popular blog involves creating valuable content on a niche topic, attracting a large audience, and generating revenue through affiliate marketing, sponsored content, advertising, and other monetization strategies.

Case Study:

Emily Jones, a lifestyle blogger, built a successful blog focusing on travel, fashion, and lifestyle topics. By partnering with affiliate programs, sponsored content collaborations, and display advertising networks, Emily monetized her blog's traffic and generated a six-figure income annually.

Getting Started:

- Choose a niche or topic for your blog based on your interests, expertise, and target audience preferences, and conduct keyword research to identify relevant content topics and search trends.

- Create high-quality, engaging content such as blog posts, articles, videos, and visuals that provide value, solve problems, or entertain your audience.
- Join affiliate marketing networks and programs relevant to your niche, promote affiliate products or services through your blog content, and earn commissions for qualified leads or sales generated through your affiliate links.
- Collaborate with brands, businesses, or advertisers for sponsored content opportunities, sponsored posts, product reviews, or brand partnerships, negotiating fees and terms that align with your audience and brand values.
- Implement monetization strategies such as display advertising, sponsored content, affiliate marketing, digital product sales, premium memberships, or crowdfunding to diversify revenue streams and maximize earnings.

22. Provide Specialized Medical or Legal Services:

Providing specialized medical or legal services involves offering expert advice, diagnosis, treatment, or legal representation in specific areas of medicine or law, catering to clients with complex or specialized needs.

Case Study:

Dr. Sarah Patel, a board-certified oncologist, established a specialized cancer care clinic offering personalized treatment plans and comprehensive support services to patients with cancer. Through her expertise, compassionate care, and multidisciplinary approach, Dr. Patel built a thriving medical practice, earning substantial income from consultations, procedures, and ancillary services.

Getting Started:
- Obtain the necessary education, training, and certifications in your chosen medical or legal specialty, acquiring specialized knowledge and skills to provide expert services to clients or patients.
- Build a professional reputation and referral network through clinical experience, research publications, speaking engagements, and collaborations with other healthcare providers or legal professionals in your field.
- Establish a private practice, clinic, or law firm specializing in your area of expertise, creating a welcoming environment, implementing efficient workflows, and offering personalized services tailored to client needs.
- Market your specialized services through targeted outreach to referring physicians, legal referrals, professional networking events, and online platforms to attract clients seeking your unique expertise and services.
- Provide exceptional care or legal representation, prioritize client/patient satisfaction, and continuously invest in ongoing education, training, and technology to stay current with advancements in your field and maintain a competitive edge.

23. Develop and Sell a Successful Online Marketplace:

Developing and selling a successful online marketplace involves creating a digital platform that connects buyers and sellers, facilitates transactions, and generates revenue through transaction fees, subscription plans, or premium services.

Case Study:

John Smith founded an online marketplace for handmade crafts and artisanal products, providing a platform for independent artisans and makers to showcase and sell their creations. By nurturing a vibrant community, ensuring trust and transparency, and offering innovative features such as virtual events and integrated payment solutions, John's online marketplace attracted millions of users and generated substantial revenue from transaction fees and premium services.

Getting Started:

- Identify a niche or vertical for your online marketplace, focusing on a specific industry, product category, geographic region, or customer segment to differentiate your platform and attract a targeted audience.
- Develop a user-friendly website or mobile app with intuitive navigation, robust search functionality, secure payment processing, and interactive features to enhance the user experience for buyers and sellers.
- Recruit sellers or merchants to onboard onto your marketplace, offering incentives such as waived fees, promotional opportunities, or value-added services to attract initial inventory and build momentum.
- Implement effective marketing and user acquisition strategies to attract buyers and sellers to your online marketplace, including search engine optimization (SEO), social media marketing, influencer partnerships, and targeted advertising campaigns.

- Continuously iterate and optimize your online marketplace based on user feedback, market trends, and performance metrics, adding new features, improving functionality, and expanding product offerings to drive growth and profitability.

24. Offer High-End Luxury Services Such as Personal Concierge or Event Planning:

Offering high-end luxury services involves providing personalized, premium services to affluent clients seeking convenience, exclusivity, and exceptional experiences, such as personal concierge services, luxury event planning, or lifestyle management.

Case Study:

Jessica White established a boutique luxury concierge and event planning agency catering to high-net-worth individuals and celebrities. By delivering white-glove service, attention to detail, and access to exclusive amenities and experiences, Jessica's agency became a trusted partner for discerning clients, earning substantial fees and commissions for their bespoke services.

Getting Started:

- Define your niche within the luxury services market, identifying areas of expertise or specialization such as personal concierge services, luxury travel planning, VIP event management, or lifestyle management.
- Establish relationships with high-net-worth individuals, affluent families, corporate executives, and entertainment

industry professionals through networking, referrals, and strategic partnerships.
- Develop a portfolio of luxury service offerings tailored to the needs and preferences of your target clientele, including personalized concierge services, bespoke travel experiences, VIP event planning, and exclusive access to premium amenities and experiences.
- Provide exceptional service and attention to detail, anticipating client needs, delivering memorable experiences, and exceeding expectations to build trust, loyalty, and repeat business.
- Cultivate a network of luxury service providers, vendors, and industry contacts to access exclusive resources, negotiate favorable terms, and enhance the value proposition for your clients.

25. Start a Successful Dropshipping Business:

Starting a successful dropshipping business involves creating an online store, sourcing products from suppliers or manufacturers, and fulfilling customer orders through third-party logistics providers without the need for inventory management or warehousing.

Case Study:

David Johnson launched a dropshipping business specializing in trendy fashion accessories and lifestyle products. By partnering with reliable suppliers, optimizing product selection, and leveraging digital marketing channels, David built a profitable e-commerce store, generating significant revenue through product sales and minimal overhead costs.

Getting Started:

- Choose a niche or product category for your dropshipping business, focusing on market demand, consumer trends, and competitive landscape to identify profitable opportunities.
- Research and identify reputable suppliers or manufacturers offering dropshipping arrangements for your chosen products, evaluating factors such as product quality, pricing, shipping times, and reliability.
- Set up an e-commerce website or utilize existing platforms such as Shopify, WooCommerce, or Amazon to create a storefront for showcasing and selling your dropshipped products, optimizing product listings, descriptions, and imagery for conversions.
- Implement digital marketing strategies such as search engine optimization (SEO), social media marketing, email marketing, and influencer partnerships to drive traffic to your dropshipping store and attract potential customers.
- Continuously monitor and optimize your dropshipping operations, including supplier relationships, product selection, pricing strategies, customer service, and order fulfillment processes, to maximize profitability and customer satisfaction.

26. Invest in Commercial Real Estate Properties:

Investing in commercial real estate properties involves acquiring income-producing assets such as office buildings, retail centers, industrial properties, or multifamily residential complexes, with the goal of generating rental income, property appreciation, and long-term wealth accumulation.

Case Study:

Emily Williams built a diverse portfolio of commercial real estate properties, including office buildings, shopping centers, and apartment complexes. Through strategic property acquisitions, proactive asset management, and leveraging financing options, Emily generated substantial cash flow, equity growth, and portfolio diversification, achieving millionaire status through her commercial real estate investments.

Getting Started:

- Conduct market research to identify promising commercial real estate markets with strong demand drivers, economic fundamentals, and growth potential in target asset classes or property sectors.
- Analyze investment opportunities based on factors such as location, property type, tenant quality, lease terms, cash flow projections, financing options, and potential for value-added improvements or redevelopment.
- Secure financing through commercial mortgages, private lenders, real estate investment partnerships, or other capital sources to fund property acquisitions and leverage investment capital.
- Implement effective property management practices to maximize occupancy rates, rental income, and property value, including tenant relations, lease negotiations, maintenance, and asset optimization strategies.
- Monitor market trends, economic indicators, and regulatory changes to identify opportunities for portfolio

optimization, asset repositioning, or strategic divestment to enhance long-term investment returns.

27. Offer High-Ticket Consulting Services to Businesses:

Offering high-ticket consulting services involves providing specialized expertise, strategic advice, and actionable recommendations to businesses seeking to solve complex challenges, improve performance, or achieve specific goals, typically commanding premium fees for your services.

Case Study:

Michael Johnson, a seasoned management consultant, established a boutique consulting firm specializing in business strategy, organizational development, and operational efficiency. By delivering tangible results, driving business growth, and demonstrating a strong return on investment for clients, Michael's consulting firm attracted high-profile clients and earned seven-figure consulting contracts.

Getting Started:

- Identify your consulting niche or area of expertise based on your industry knowledge, skills, and experience, focusing on specific sectors, functions, or strategic objectives where you can provide significant value to clients.
- Define your consulting services and value proposition, emphasizing your unique approach, methodology, and track record of delivering measurable results and business impact for clients.

- Develop a compelling brand identity, website, and marketing materials that showcase your expertise, case studies, client testimonials, and thought leadership content to establish credibility and attract prospective clients.
- Network and build relationships with potential clients, industry influencers, and referral partners through speaking engagements, industry events, professional associations, and online platforms to generate leads and referrals.
- Deliver exceptional consulting services, tailored solutions, and actionable insights that address client needs, solve problems, and drive business outcomes, exceeding client expectations and fostering long-term relationships and repeat business.

28. Develop and Sell a Successful Mobile Game:

Developing and selling a successful mobile game involves creating engaging, addictive gameplay experiences, leveraging innovative mechanics, captivating storytelling, and immersive visuals to attract and retain players, and monetizing your game through in-app purchases, advertising, or premium downloads.

Case Study:

Sarah Jackson, an independent game developer, created a popular mobile game that went viral, attracting millions of downloads and generating substantial revenue from in-app purchases and advertising. By focusing on player engagement, user feedback, and continuous updates, Sarah's mobile game became a commercial success, earning her millions of dollars in annual revenue.

Getting Started:

- Identify a game concept or idea that has market potential, considering factors such as target audience preferences, genre trends, platform compatibility, and monetization opportunities.
- Develop a prototype or minimum viable product (MVP) to test gameplay mechanics, user experience, and technical feasibility, gathering feedback from beta testers, focus groups, or early adopters to refine your game design.
- Build your mobile game using game development tools, software libraries, and programming languages suited to your platform of choice (iOS, Android, or cross-platform), ensuring high performance, scalability, and compatibility with target devices.
- Implement monetization features such as in-app purchases, rewarded ads, premium upgrades, or subscription plans strategically within your game, balancing player engagement with revenue generation to optimize monetization potential.
- Launch and promote your mobile game through app stores, social media, influencer marketing, press releases, and promotional campaigns to reach your target audience, drive downloads, and maximize visibility and discoverability.

29. Start a Successful SaaS (Software as a Service) Business:

Starting a successful SaaS (Software as a Service) business involves developing a cloud-based software solution that solves a specific problem or addresses a market need, delivering value through subscription-based pricing models, and scaling your business through customer acquisition and retention.

Case Study:

John Smith co-founded a SaaS startup offering project management software for small businesses. By building an intuitive, feature-rich platform, providing exceptional customer support, and executing targeted marketing and sales strategies, John's SaaS business achieved rapid growth, attracting thousands of subscribers and generating millions of dollars in recurring revenue.

Getting Started:

- Identify a market opportunity or pain point that can be addressed with a software solution, conducting market research, customer interviews, and competitive analysis to validate demand and identify target customers.
- Develop a scalable and user-friendly SaaS product, focusing on core features, usability, reliability, and security, and leveraging agile development methodologies to iterate and improve based on user feedback and market trends.
- Define your pricing strategy, subscription plans, and pricing tiers based on value metrics, customer segmentation, and competitive benchmarking, offering

free trials, freemium models, or tiered pricing options to attract and retain customers.
- Build a go-to-market strategy encompassing product launch, marketing campaigns, lead generation, sales outreach, and customer onboarding to acquire early adopters and drive initial traction and revenue growth.
- Continuously iterate and innovate your SaaS product based on customer feedback, usage data, and market insights, expanding feature sets, improving performance, and staying ahead of competitors to retain customers and drive long-term success.

30. **Provide High-End Graphic Design or Branding Services:**

Providing high-end graphic design or branding services involves delivering premium design solutions, creative assets, and brand identity packages to clients seeking professional visual communication, brand differentiation, and market positioning.

Case Study:

Samantha Roberts established a boutique graphic design agency specializing in branding, logo design, and visual identity development for luxury brands and high-end clientele. By combining artistic creativity, strategic thinking, and meticulous attention to detail, Samantha's agency became a trusted partner for luxury businesses, earning substantial fees for their premium design services.

Getting Started:

- Showcase your design portfolio, expertise, and unique design style through a professional website, online portfolio, social media profiles, and design showcases to attract potential clients and demonstrate your capabilities.
- Identify your target market and ideal clients, focusing on industries, sectors, or businesses that value high-quality design, creativity, and brand aesthetics, such as fashion, hospitality, beauty, or luxury goods.
- Offer a range of graphic design services tailored to client needs, including logo design, brand identity development, packaging design, marketing collateral, website design, and digital assets, emphasizing your ability to deliver cohesive and impactful brand experiences.
- Provide exceptional client service, consultation, and collaboration throughout the design process, from initial concept development and ideation to final deliverables, revisions, and implementation, ensuring client satisfaction and project success.
- Cultivate long-term relationships with clients, earning their trust, loyalty, and referrals through consistently delivering outstanding design work, exceeding expectations, and contributing to their business growth and success.

31. Become a Successful Freelance Writer or Copywriter:

Becoming a successful freelance writer or copywriter involves leveraging your writing skills, expertise, and creativity to craft compelling content, articles, copy, or marketing materials for clients across various industries, earning income through freelance assignments, contracts, or royalties.

Case Study:

Jessica Davis built a thriving freelance writing business, specializing in content marketing, blog writing, and copywriting services for B2B clients. By delivering high-quality, SEO-optimized content, meeting deadlines, and building a strong reputation for reliability and professionalism, Jessica attracted premium clients and achieved six-figure earnings as a freelance writer.

Getting Started:

- Showcase your writing portfolio, samples, and expertise in a professional website, online portfolio, or freelance marketplace profile to attract potential clients and demonstrate your writing style, voice, and versatility.
- Identify your niche or specialization within the freelance writing market, such as technology, finance, healthcare, lifestyle, or travel, based on your interests, expertise, and target audience preferences.
- Network and prospect for clients through freelance platforms, job boards, industry forums, social media groups, and professional associations, pitching your services, submitting proposals, and responding to job postings to secure freelance assignments and projects.
- Deliver high-quality writing services tailored to client needs, meeting project requirements, deadlines, and quality standards, while maintaining open communication, addressing feedback, and ensuring client satisfaction to foster long-term relationships and repeat business.

- Continuously refine and expand your writing skills, stay informed about industry trends, writing best practices, and content marketing strategies, and seek opportunities for professional development, training, and mentorship to enhance your expertise and marketability as a freelance writer.

32. Offer High-End Interior Design or Architectural Services:

Offering high-end interior design or architectural services involves creating custom, luxury design solutions for residential, commercial, or hospitality projects, catering to affluent clients seeking bespoke, sophisticated, and aesthetically pleasing environments.

Case Study:

Michael Thompson established an award-winning interior design firm specializing in luxury residential projects and high-end hospitality spaces. By combining innovative design concepts, exquisite craftsmanship, and attention to detail, Michael's firm attracted high-profile clients and earned prestigious commissions for luxury properties, generating significant revenue and industry acclaim.

Getting Started:

- Showcase your design portfolio, expertise, and signature style through a professional website, design portfolio, social media platforms, and industry publications to showcase your talent and attract potential clients.

- Define your target market and ideal clients, focusing on affluent homeowners, real estate developers, boutique hotels, luxury retailers, or high-end restaurants seeking distinctive design solutions and personalized service.
- Offer comprehensive interior design or architectural services tailored to client preferences, including conceptual design, space planning, material selection, custom furnishings, lighting design, and project management, emphasizing your ability to deliver exceptional craftsmanship, quality, and luxury.
- Cultivate relationships with architects, builders, craftsmen, artisans, and suppliers to access premium materials, finishes, and resources, collaborating with trusted partners to execute design projects with precision and excellence.
- Provide exceptional client service, communication, and collaboration throughout the design process, from initial consultations and concept presentations to final installations, ensuring client satisfaction and exceeding expectations for luxury and elegance.

33. Invest in Precious Metals Such as Gold or Silver:

Investing in precious metals such as gold or silver involves acquiring physical bullion, coins, or exchange-traded products (ETPs) as a store of value, inflation hedge, portfolio diversifier, or safe haven asset, with the potential for long-term capital appreciation and wealth preservation.

Case Study:

David Johnson diversified his investment portfolio by allocating a portion of his assets to physical gold and silver holdings. By recognizing the intrinsic value, scarcity, and historical significance of precious metals, David protected his wealth against currency devaluation, geopolitical risks, and economic uncertainty, while benefiting from price appreciation during periods of market volatility and inflation.

Getting Started:
- Educate yourself about the fundamentals of precious metals investing, including supply and demand dynamics, market drivers, historical performance, and the role of gold and silver as alternative assets in a diversified investment portfolio.
- Determine your investment objectives, risk tolerance, and time horizon for investing in precious metals, considering factors such as wealth preservation, portfolio diversification, inflation protection, or speculation on price movements.
- Choose a suitable investment vehicle or method for acquiring precious metals, such as physical bullion bars or coins, allocated or unallocated storage accounts, exchange-traded funds (ETFs), or precious metal mining stocks, based on your preferences, liquidity needs, and storage options.
- Develop a disciplined investment strategy and asset allocation plan for incorporating precious metals into your overall portfolio, setting allocation targets, rebalancing periodically, and monitoring market conditions, economic trends, and geopolitical developments that may impact precious metal prices.

- Secure and store your precious metal holdings safely and securely, utilizing reputable dealers, custodians, or storage facilities, and implementing appropriate security measures to protect your investment from theft, loss, or damage.

34. Start a Successful Affiliate Marketing Business:

Starting a successful affiliate marketing business involves promoting third-party products or services through affiliate links or referral codes, earning commissions for qualified sales, leads, or actions generated through your marketing efforts, leveraging digital platforms, content creation, and audience engagement.

Case Study:

Rachel Miller launched an affiliate marketing business focused on promoting beauty and skincare products through her blog and social media channels. By creating authentic, engaging content, building trust with her audience, and strategically integrating affiliate links into her recommendations and reviews, Rachel generated passive income streams and earned commissions from affiliate partnerships.

Getting Started:

- Choose a niche or product category for your affiliate marketing business based on your interests, expertise, and target audience preferences, identifying affiliate programs and products that align with your niche and offer competitive commissions.

- Build an online platform or content hub such as a blog, website, YouTube channel, podcast, or social media profile to create and share valuable content, product reviews, tutorials, recommendations, or promotional campaigns that drive traffic and conversions for affiliate partners.
- Join reputable affiliate marketing networks, programs, or platforms such as Amazon Associates, ClickBank, ShareASale, or CJ Affiliate to access a wide range of affiliate offers, tracking tools, reporting analytics, and payment processing services.
- Implement effective content marketing, SEO, email marketing, social media marketing, and other digital marketing strategies to attract and engage your target audience, drive traffic to affiliate offers, and maximize conversion rates and affiliate earnings.
- Monitor performance metrics, track affiliate sales, clicks, and commissions, analyze campaign effectiveness, and optimize your marketing efforts based on data insights, user feedback, and market trends to continuously improve your affiliate marketing business.

35. Offer Specialized IT or Cybersecurity Consulting Services:

Offering specialized IT or cybersecurity consulting services involves providing expert advice, solutions, and support to businesses, organizations, or individuals seeking to safeguard their digital assets, mitigate cybersecurity risks, and optimize their IT infrastructure, systems, and processes.

Case Study:

Mark Johnson founded a cybersecurity consulting firm specializing in penetration testing, vulnerability assessments, and incident response services for small and medium-sized enterprises (SMEs). By identifying security vulnerabilities, implementing proactive measures, and educating clients on best practices, Mark's firm helped businesses strengthen their cyber defenses, protect sensitive data, and comply with regulatory requirements, earning substantial fees for their specialized services.

Getting Started:

- Acquire relevant certifications, credentials, and training in IT security, cybersecurity, network infrastructure, risk management, and compliance standards such as CISSP, CISA, CEH, or CompTIA Security+ to demonstrate your expertise and credibility as a cybersecurity consultant.
- Identify your target market and ideal clients, focusing on industries or sectors with specific cybersecurity needs, regulatory obligations, or compliance requirements such as finance, healthcare, government, or e-commerce.
- Develop a comprehensive suite of cybersecurity services tailored to client needs, including risk assessments, security audits, policy development, incident response planning, security awareness training, and regulatory compliance assistance, emphasizing your ability to address cybersecurity challenges holistically.
- Market your cybersecurity consulting services through targeted outreach, thought leadership content, speaking engagements, industry conferences, and strategic partnerships to raise awareness, generate leads, and

establish yourself as a trusted advisor and cybersecurity expert.
- Deliver high-value consulting engagements, solutions, and recommendations that align with client goals, objectives, and risk tolerance, providing actionable insights, remediation strategies, and ongoing support to enhance cybersecurity posture and resilience.

36. Develop and Sell a Successful Online Fitness Program:

Developing and selling a successful online fitness program involves creating digital workout routines, training plans, nutrition guides, or wellness programs, delivering value, motivation, and accountability to clients seeking convenient, accessible, and effective fitness solutions.

Case Study:

Sarah Smith launched an online fitness platform offering personalized workout programs, live coaching sessions, and nutritional support to subscribers worldwide. By leveraging technology, social media, and digital marketing channels, Sarah reached a global audience, built a loyal community of fitness enthusiasts, and generated recurring revenue through subscription-based memberships and digital product sales.

Getting Started:
- Identify your target audience and niche within the online fitness market, such as weight loss, muscle gain, endurance training, yoga, or holistic wellness, based on your expertise, passion, and competitive advantage.

- Develop high-quality fitness content, including workout videos, exercise routines, meal plans, recipes, progress trackers, and educational resources, tailored to the needs, goals, and fitness levels of your target audience, emphasizing convenience, variety, and results.
- Choose a digital platform or membership site to host your online fitness program, leveraging features such as video hosting, payment processing, member management, community forums, and content delivery to create a seamless user experience for your subscribers.
- Market your online fitness program through social media, influencer partnerships, email marketing, content marketing, and online advertising to attract new subscribers, engage your audience, and drive conversions, offering free trials, discounts, or incentives to encourage sign-ups.
- Provide ongoing support, motivation, and accountability to your online fitness community, engaging with members, answering questions, providing feedback, and fostering a supportive and encouraging environment to help them achieve their health and fitness goals.

37. Provide Specialized Financial Planning or Wealth Management Services:

Providing specialized financial planning or wealth management services involves offering personalized investment advice, retirement planning, estate planning, tax optimization, and wealth preservation strategies to affluent individuals, families, or businesses seeking to build and protect their financial assets.

Case Study:

Emily Johnson established a boutique wealth management firm catering to high-net-worth clients, providing comprehensive financial planning, investment management, and wealth advisory services. By delivering customized solutions, holistic advice, and superior client service, Emily's firm attracted affluent clientele and achieved significant growth in assets under management, generating substantial revenue and advisory fees.

Getting Started:

- Obtain relevant certifications, licenses, and credentials in financial planning, investment management, or wealth advisory services, such as CFP (Certified Financial Planner), CFA (Chartered Financial Analyst), or ChFC (Chartered Financial Consultant), to demonstrate your expertise and credibility.
- Define your target market and ideal clients, focusing on individuals, families, or businesses with complex financial needs, substantial assets, or specific wealth management objectives, such as retirement planning, estate planning, tax optimization, or legacy preservation.
- Develop a comprehensive suite of financial planning services tailored to client goals, risk tolerance, time horizon, and financial circumstances, including investment analysis, asset allocation, risk management, tax planning, retirement income planning, and wealth transfer strategies.
- Build relationships and trust with clients through personalized consultations, financial assessments, goal setting, and ongoing reviews, providing transparent

advice, education, and guidance to help clients make informed decisions and achieve their financial objectives.
- Continuously monitor and review client portfolios, economic trends, market conditions, and regulatory changes, adjusting investment strategies, asset allocations, and financial plans as needed to adapt to changing circumstances and optimize client outcomes.

38. Invest in Blue-Chip Stocks with a Proven Track Record:

Investing in blue-chip stocks with a proven track record involves acquiring shares of established, reputable companies with strong financial performance, market leadership, and sustainable competitive advantages, aiming for long-term capital appreciation, dividend income, and portfolio stability.

Case Study:

David Williams built a diversified investment portfolio consisting of blue-chip stocks from reputable companies across various sectors such as technology, healthcare, consumer goods, and finance. By focusing on quality, stability, and growth potential, David achieved consistent returns, dividend income, and wealth accumulation over time, leveraging the resilience and proven track record of blue-chip investments.

Getting Started:

- Research and analyze blue-chip stocks based on fundamental criteria such as earnings growth, revenue stability, dividend history, market share, brand

recognition, and competitive positioning, identifying companies with strong financials, durable business models, and shareholder-friendly policies.
- Diversify your portfolio across different industries, sectors, and geographic regions to mitigate risk and capture opportunities for growth and income generation, balancing stability with growth potential in your stock selection.
- Monitor and track the performance of blue-chip stocks, staying informed about company news, earnings reports, industry trends, and market developments that may impact stock prices, dividend payouts, or long-term investment prospects.
- Invest for the long term, adopting a buy-and-hold strategy with a focus on capital preservation, compounding returns, and dividend reinvestment, resisting the temptation to react to short-term market fluctuations or noise, and maintaining discipline and patience in your investment approach.
- Review and rebalance your portfolio periodically to ensure alignment with your investment goals, risk tolerance, and financial objectives, making adjustments as needed based on changes in market conditions, economic outlook, or personal circumstances.

39. Start a Successful Clothing Line or Fashion Brand:

Starting a successful clothing line or fashion brand involves designing, producing, and marketing apparel, accessories, or footwear that resonate with target consumers, reflect brand identity and aesthetic, and offer unique value propositions or style statements in the fashion marketplace.

Case Study:

Emma Thompson launched her own fashion brand specializing in sustainable, ethically sourced clothing made from organic materials. By emphasizing environmental consciousness, social responsibility, and timeless design, Emma's clothing line gained traction among eco-conscious consumers and fashion enthusiasts, earning recognition and loyalty for its commitment to sustainability and style.

Getting Started:

- Identify your niche, target audience, and brand positioning within the fashion market, considering factors such as style preferences, lifestyle trends, demographic profiles, and competitive landscape to differentiate your clothing line and appeal to specific consumer segments.
- Develop a distinctive brand identity, visual aesthetic, and brand story that align with your values, mission, and target audience, conveying authenticity, creativity, and relevance through brand messaging, imagery, and marketing materials.
- Create compelling, trend-forward designs and product offerings that capture the essence of your brand, incorporating quality craftsmanship, innovative fabrics, and thoughtful details to enhance perceived value and desirability among consumers.
- Establish reliable supply chain partnerships, production capabilities, and manufacturing processes to ensure consistent quality, timely delivery, and cost efficiency in

producing your clothing line, balancing design creativity with production feasibility and scalability.
- Launch and promote your clothing line through multi-channel marketing strategies, including e-commerce platforms, social media marketing, influencer collaborations, pop-up events, and fashion shows, building brand awareness, generating buzz, and driving sales conversions among your target audience.

40. Offer Specialized Marketing or Advertising Services:

Offering specialized marketing or advertising services involves providing strategic consulting, creative solutions, and campaign management to businesses, brands, or agencies seeking to optimize their marketing efforts, reach target audiences, and achieve marketing objectives.

Case Study:

Alex Johnson founded a boutique marketing agency specializing in digital advertising and social media marketing for small and medium-sized businesses. By leveraging data-driven insights, creative storytelling, and targeted ad campaigns, Alex's agency helped clients increase brand visibility, drive website traffic, and generate qualified leads, delivering measurable results and ROI for their marketing investments.

Getting Started:
- Define your area of specialization within the marketing or advertising industry, such as digital marketing, social

media advertising, content marketing, influencer marketing, or search engine optimization (SEO), based on your expertise, interests, and market demand.
- Build a strong portfolio showcasing your past work, successful campaigns, case studies, and client testimonials to demonstrate your expertise, creativity, and proven track record in delivering results-driven marketing solutions.
- Identify your target market and ideal clients, focusing on specific industries, sectors, or business sizes that align with your expertise and value proposition, such as e-commerce brands, tech startups, healthcare providers, or local businesses.
- Offer a range of specialized marketing services tailored to client needs, objectives, and budget constraints, providing strategic planning, campaign execution, performance analysis, and optimization recommendations to drive maximum impact and ROI for clients' marketing investments.
- Invest in continuous learning, professional development, and staying abreast of industry trends, emerging technologies, and best practices in marketing and advertising, to innovate, differentiate, and maintain a competitive edge in the marketplace.

41. Invest in Art or Collectibles with Potential for Appreciation:

Investing in art or collectibles with potential for appreciation involves acquiring valuable artworks, rare collectibles, or unique cultural artifacts as tangible assets, diversifying investment portfolios, and capturing potential capital gains or cultural value appreciation over time.

Case Study:

Jonathan Carter diversified his investment portfolio by allocating a portion of his assets to fine art and collectible assets, including paintings, sculptures, and vintage collectibles. By leveraging expertise, research, and market insights, Jonathan identified undervalued artworks and niche collectibles with potential for appreciation, building a valuable art collection that served as both an investment and a passion.

Getting Started:

- Educate yourself about the art market, collectibles markets, art history, provenance, authenticity, and valuation methods to make informed investment decisions, understand market trends, and identify opportunities for potential appreciation.
- Determine your investment objectives, risk tolerance, and budget for acquiring art or collectibles, considering factors such as liquidity, storage costs, insurance, and potential market volatility associated with alternative assets.
- Research and analyze artworks, artists, art movements, or collectible categories that interest you, seeking expert advice, appraisals, and due diligence to assess authenticity, condition, provenance, and investment potential before making acquisitions.
- Build relationships with art dealers, galleries, auction houses, and collectors to access exclusive opportunities, negotiate favorable terms, and stay informed about

- upcoming auctions, private sales, or exhibitions that may offer desirable pieces for investment.
- Manage and maintain your art or collectible investments carefully, documenting purchases, keeping records of provenance and transactions, ensuring proper conservation and preservation measures, and periodically reviewing your collection's performance and market value.

42. Develop and Sell a Successful Online Dating Platform:

Developing and selling a successful online dating platform involves creating a user-friendly, feature-rich dating website or mobile app that connects singles, facilitates meaningful connections, and offers unique value propositions or niche targeting to attract and retain users in a competitive market.

Case Study:

Julia Evans founded a niche online dating platform catering to professionals seeking serious relationships and meaningful connections. By focusing on compatibility matching, personalized matchmaking, and stringent verification processes, Julia's dating platform gained popularity among career-oriented singles, achieving rapid user growth and monetization through subscription-based memberships.

Getting Started:

- Identify your target audience and niche within the online dating market, such as age group, demographic profile, relationship preferences, lifestyle interests, or cultural

background, based on market research, competitor analysis, and user insights.
- Develop a comprehensive business plan outlining your dating platform's features, functionality, user experience, monetization strategy, marketing approach, and growth projections, ensuring alignment with target audience needs and market trends.
- Design and develop your online dating platform using reliable technology, user-friendly interfaces, intuitive navigation, and robust security measures to create a safe, engaging, and trustworthy dating environment for users.
- Launch and promote your dating platform through digital marketing channels, social media campaigns, influencer partnerships, affiliate programs, and targeted advertising to attract an initial user base, encourage user engagement, and drive membership sign-ups.
- Continuously optimize and evolve your dating platform based on user feedback, analytics, and market dynamics, implementing new features, refining matchmaking algorithms, and addressing user needs to enhance user satisfaction, retention, and revenue generation.

43. Offer Specialized Coaching or Training for Athletes or Performers:

Offering specialized coaching or training for athletes or performers involves providing personalized instruction, skill development, and performance enhancement techniques to help individuals excel in their chosen sport, art form, or creative endeavor, leveraging expertise, experience, and tailored programs.

Case Study:

Sarah Johnson established a boutique coaching practice specializing in elite-level gymnastics training for aspiring athletes. By combining technical expertise, biomechanical analysis, and mental conditioning techniques, Sarah helped gymnasts improve their skills, overcome challenges, and achieve competitive success, earning recognition as a top coach in the field.

Getting Started:

- Identify your area of expertise, specialization, or coaching niche within the sports or performing arts industry, such as gymnastics, dance, martial arts, tennis, music, acting, or public speaking, based on your background, skills, and passion.
- Obtain relevant certifications, qualifications, or credentials in coaching, sports science, performance psychology, or teaching pedagogy to enhance your credibility, knowledge, and professional standing as a coach or trainer.
- Develop customized coaching programs, lesson plans, and training protocols tailored to individual athletes' or performers' goals, abilities, and developmental needs, incorporating technical instruction, skill drills, conditioning exercises, and performance assessments.
- Establish a coaching studio, training facility, or virtual coaching platform equipped with necessary equipment, resources, and technology to deliver effective coaching sessions, demonstrations, and feedback in a supportive and conducive environment.

- Promote your coaching services through targeted marketing, networking, referrals, and partnerships with sports clubs, schools, academies, or talent agencies to attract clients, build rapport, and demonstrate your value as a coach or trainer.

44. Invest in Dividend-Paying Stocks for Steady Income:

Investing in dividend-paying stocks for steady income involves acquiring shares of publicly traded companies that distribute regular dividends to shareholders, providing a reliable stream of passive income, potential capital appreciation, and portfolio stability over the long term.

Case Study:

Michael Smith built a diversified investment portfolio focused on dividend-paying stocks from reputable companies with strong financial fundamentals, consistent dividend histories, and sustainable payout ratios. By reinvesting dividends, compounding returns, and strategically rebalancing his portfolio, Michael generated a steady stream of passive income while preserving capital and achieving long-term wealth accumulation.

Getting Started:

- Research and select dividend-paying stocks based on criteria such as dividend yield, dividend growth rate, payout ratio, earnings stability, cash flow generation, and industry outlook, focusing on companies with a track

record of reliable dividend payments and potential for future growth.
- Diversify your dividend stock holdings across different sectors, industries, and market capitalizations to mitigate risk and capture opportunities for income generation, capital appreciation, and portfolio diversification, avoiding overexposure to any single stock or sector.
- Monitor and analyze dividend stocks' performance, financial health, dividend sustainability, and market trends, conducting due diligence, reviewing earnings reports, and staying informed about company developments that may impact dividend policies or shareholder returns.
- Reinvest dividends automatically through dividend reinvestment plans (DRIPs) or manually allocate dividends to purchase additional shares, leveraging the power of compounding to accelerate wealth accumulation and increase future income streams from dividend stocks.
- Review and adjust your dividend stock portfolio periodically based on changes in your investment objectives, risk tolerance, market conditions, and economic outlook, rebalancing asset allocation and dividend reinvestment strategies to optimize income generation and capital growth.

45. Start a Successful Food Delivery Service or Meal Prep Business:

Starting a successful food delivery service or meal prep business involves offering convenient, healthy, and customizable meal options delivered directly to customers' homes or workplaces, leveraging digital platforms, culinary expertise, and operational efficiency to meet consumer demand for convenience and quality.

Case Study:

John Davis launched a meal prep delivery service specializing in nutritious, chef-prepared meals tailored to customers' dietary preferences and health goals. By partnering with local suppliers, optimizing kitchen operations, and leveraging technology for online ordering and delivery logistics, John's business gained popularity among busy professionals, fitness enthusiasts, and health-conscious consumers, generating recurring revenue and loyal customers.

Getting Started:

- Identify your target market and niche within the food delivery or meal prep industry, such as busy professionals, fitness enthusiasts, families, seniors, or individuals with dietary restrictions, based on consumer preferences, market trends, and competitive analysis.
- Develop a menu of healthy, delicious, and customizable meal options featuring fresh ingredients, balanced nutrition, and diverse flavors to appeal to your target audience's tastes, dietary preferences, and lifestyle needs.
- Establish efficient kitchen facilities, food preparation processes, and supply chain partnerships to ensure quality control, consistency, and scalability in producing and delivering meals to customers, adhering to food safety standards and regulations.
- Build a user-friendly online ordering platform, mobile app, or subscription service for customers to browse

menus, place orders, customize meal plans, schedule deliveries, and manage subscriptions, providing convenience, flexibility, and personalization in their ordering experience.

- Implement effective marketing and promotional strategies to attract customers, drive sales, and build brand awareness through social media marketing, influencer partnerships, email campaigns, referral programs, and local advertising, highlighting the value proposition, quality, and convenience of your food delivery service or meal prep offerings.

46. Offer Specialized Language Translation or Interpretation Services:

Offering specialized language translation or interpretation services involves providing accurate, culturally sensitive, and timely language solutions for individuals, businesses, or organizations seeking to communicate effectively across linguistic and cultural barriers, leveraging linguistic expertise, cultural knowledge, and technology tools.

Case Study:

Maria Lopez founded a language services agency specializing in professional translation and interpretation services for multinational corporations, government agencies, and non-profit organizations. By assembling a team of skilled linguists, subject matter experts, and industry specialists, Maria's agency delivered high-quality language solutions in multiple languages, sectors, and industries, earning trust, credibility, and repeat business from clients worldwide.

Getting Started:

- Identify your language pairs, specialization areas, and target markets within the language services industry, such as legal, medical, technical, business, or literary translation, based on your language skills, expertise, and market demand.
- Obtain relevant certifications, qualifications, or credentials in translation, interpretation, or language proficiency, such as ATA (American Translators Association) certification, court certification, or language proficiency tests, to demonstrate your competence and professionalism as a language service provider.
- Invest in technology tools, translation software, and CAT (Computer-Assisted Translation) tools to streamline workflow, improve productivity, and ensure consistency and accuracy in translation projects, leveraging terminology databases, glossaries, and translation memory for efficiency and quality assurance.
- Build relationships with clients, agencies, and industry contacts through networking, referrals, and online platforms, showcasing your language expertise, specialization areas, and track record of successful projects to attract new clients, secure contracts, and expand your client base.
- Provide exceptional customer service, communication, and project management throughout the translation process, maintaining transparency, responsiveness, and professionalism in client interactions, delivering high-quality translations on time and within budget, and soliciting feedback to continuously improve service quality and client satisfaction.

47. Develop and Sell a Successful Mobile Productivity App:

Developing and selling a successful mobile productivity app involves creating a user-friendly, feature-rich application designed to enhance users' efficiency, organization, and productivity in various aspects of their personal or professional lives, leveraging technology, usability, and value proposition to attract users and generate revenue.

Case Study:

Adam Smith developed a mobile productivity app designed to streamline task management, time tracking, and project collaboration for small businesses and freelancers. By prioritizing user experience, intuitive design, and robust functionality, Adam's app gained popularity among busy professionals, remote teams, and entrepreneurs, achieving high user ratings, positive reviews, and steady revenue from premium subscriptions and in-app purchases.

Getting Started:

- Identify a niche or pain point within the productivity software market, such as task management, note-taking, calendar organization, document collaboration, or workflow automation, based on user needs, competitor analysis, and market research.
- Define your app's core features, functionality, and unique selling points (USPs), focusing on usability, simplicity, and effectiveness in addressing users' productivity challenges, while differentiating your app from existing solutions in the marketplace.

- Design a user-friendly interface, intuitive navigation, and visually appealing aesthetics for your mobile app, following best practices in mobile app design, user experience (UX) design, and human-computer interaction (HCI) principles to enhance usability and engagement.
- Develop a scalable, reliable, and secure mobile app using modern development frameworks, programming languages, and cloud-based infrastructure, ensuring compatibility across different devices, platforms, and screen sizes, and optimizing performance, responsiveness, and data privacy.
- Launch and market your mobile productivity app through app stores, digital platforms, social media channels, and targeted advertising campaigns to reach your target audience, generate downloads, and acquire users, while continuously iterating, updating, and enhancing your app based on user feedback, analytics, and market trends.

48. Invest in Emerging Markets with High Growth Potential:

Investing in emerging markets with high growth potential involves allocating capital to stocks, bonds, or funds that represent companies or economies in developing or transitional stages, aiming to capture superior returns, diversify investment portfolios, and capitalize on long-term growth opportunities in dynamic, expanding markets.

Case Study:

Sophia Patel diversified her investment portfolio by allocating a portion of her assets to emerging market equities, bonds, and exchange-traded funds (ETFs) focused on regions such as Asia, Latin America, and Africa. By leveraging research, market analysis, and asset allocation strategies, Sophia benefited from the rapid economic growth, demographic trends, and structural transformations driving emerging market investments, achieving attractive returns and portfolio growth over time.

Getting Started:

- Conduct thorough research and analysis of emerging market opportunities, considering factors such as economic growth prospects, political stability, demographic trends, technological advancements, regulatory environment, and market valuations to identify promising investment themes, sectors, or regions.
- Diversify your investments across different emerging markets, asset classes, and investment vehicles to spread risk, capture opportunities, and mitigate volatility, combining equities, bonds, currencies, and alternative investments to achieve a balanced portfolio allocation.
- Invest through diversified mutual funds, ETFs, or index funds that track broad-based or sector-specific emerging market indices, providing exposure to a basket of stocks or bonds across multiple countries and industries, with professional management and risk diversification benefits.
- Stay informed about global macroeconomic trends, geopolitical developments, currency fluctuations, and market risks that may impact emerging market

investments, conducting due diligence, monitoring portfolio performance, and adjusting asset allocation as needed to manage risk and optimize returns.

- Adopt a long-term investment horizon, patience, and discipline in navigating emerging market opportunities, recognizing the potential for higher volatility, market cycles, and geopolitical risks inherent in developing economies, while focusing on the fundamental growth drivers and structural trends shaping long-term investment prospects.

49. Start a Successful Pet Care or Grooming Business:

Starting a successful pet care or grooming business involves providing professional grooming, boarding, training, or daycare services for pets, catering to pet owners' needs for convenience, quality, and care for their beloved animals, while creating a rewarding and profitable business venture.

Case Study:

Emily Thompson established a boutique pet grooming salon offering premium grooming services for dogs and cats, including baths, haircuts, nail trimming, and spa treatments. By focusing on personalized service, gentle handling, and quality grooming products, Emily's salon attracted a loyal clientele of pet owners seeking top-notch care and grooming for their furry companions, achieving steady revenue growth and positive word-of-mouth referrals.

Getting Started:

- Identify your target market and niche within the pet care industry, such as grooming, boarding, training, daycare, or specialty services for specific pet breeds, sizes, or needs, based on local demand, competition, and your expertise or passion for working with animals.
- Obtain necessary licenses, permits, and certifications required to operate a pet care or grooming business in your area, ensuring compliance with regulatory requirements, health and safety standards, and animal welfare regulations.
- Set up a professional grooming salon or pet care facility equipped with grooming tools, supplies, and amenities tailored to pets' comfort, safety, and hygiene, creating a welcoming and stress-free environment for both pets and their owners.
- Hire qualified groomers, pet care professionals, or certified trainers to deliver high-quality services, compassionate care, and personalized attention to pets, ensuring staff training, supervision, and ongoing education to maintain service excellence and customer satisfaction.
- Market and promote your pet care or grooming business through local advertising, community outreach, social media marketing, and partnerships with pet-related businesses, veterinarians, pet stores, or animal rescue organizations, showcasing your expertise, reputation, and commitment to pet welfare.

50. Offer Specialized Engineering or Technical Consulting Services:

Offering specialized engineering or technical consulting services involves providing expert advice, solutions, and project support in specialized fields of engineering, technology, or scientific disciplines to help clients solve complex problems, optimize processes, and achieve business objectives, leveraging technical expertise, analytical skills, and industry knowledge.

Case Study:

Matthew Harris established an engineering consulting firm specializing in renewable energy systems design and implementation. By offering comprehensive consulting services, feasibility studies, and project management support for solar, wind, and biomass energy projects, Matthew's firm helped clients navigate regulatory requirements, assess investment opportunities, and implement sustainable energy solutions, contributing to environmental impact reduction and economic growth.

Getting Started:

- Define your area of specialization within the engineering or technical consulting industry, such as civil engineering, mechanical engineering, electrical engineering, environmental engineering, software development, cybersecurity, or data analytics, based on your expertise, qualifications, and market demand.
- Identify target clients and industries that require specialized engineering or technical expertise, such as government agencies, private corporations, research institutions, or non-profit organizations, focusing on

sectors with complex challenges, regulatory compliance needs, or technological advancements.
- Develop a portfolio of consulting services, solutions, and deliverables tailored to client needs, project requirements, and industry standards, offering services such as technical assessments, feasibility studies, design engineering, system integration, troubleshooting, and regulatory compliance support.
- Build relationships and partnerships with industry stakeholders, professional associations, academic institutions, and technology vendors to stay updated on industry trends, emerging technologies, and best practices, while expanding your network, visibility, and credibility as a trusted advisor and subject matter expert.
- Promote your engineering or technical consulting services through targeted marketing, thought leadership content, speaking engagements, and networking events, demonstrating your expertise, problem-solving skills, and track record of successful projects to attract clients, build trust, and secure consulting engagements.

Congratulations! You've reached the 50th way to make a million dollars a year! Your commitment to exploring these strategies demonstrates your ambition and determination to achieve financial success. Keep believing in yourself, keep pursuing your dreams, and keep taking action. Striving for a million-dollar income requires more than mere ambition; it necessitates disciplined time management. Maximize each moment, stay resolute in your pursuits, and let your steadfast dedication to success propel you toward unparalleled financial success. Through my entrepreneurship journey, I'd often fallen into a loop of overconsumption of material. Whether it be entertainment or information, both are equally detrimental in their excess. Quit overconsumption now and take the first step. It's only a matter of time before someone else implements your good idea. Success involves putting one foot in front of the other each day... and conducting thorough market research! 1,700 people become millionaires every day in the US alone. Choose your day, and work towards it.

51. Develop and Sell a Successful Online Productivity Tool:

Developing and selling a successful online productivity tool involves creating a digital solution, software, or application designed to enhance users' efficiency, organization, and collaboration in managing tasks, projects, and workflows, leveraging technology, user feedback, and market demand to deliver value and generate revenue.

Case Study:

Samantha Lee developed a web-based project management tool tailored to remote teams and freelancers, offering features such as task tracking, time management, file sharing, and team collaboration. By addressing pain points and usability issues in existing tools, Samantha's productivity tool gained traction among remote workers, small businesses, and startups, attracting paying subscribers and recurring revenue.

Getting Started:

- Identify a niche or problem within the productivity software market, such as project management, task

tracking, time tracking, team communication, or workflow automation, based on user feedback, competitor analysis, and market research.
- Define your tool's unique value proposition, core features, and user experience, focusing on simplicity, usability, and effectiveness in addressing users' productivity challenges, while differentiating your tool from competitors in the marketplace.
- Design and develop your online productivity tool using modern web development technologies, agile methodologies, and user-centered design principles, iterating on prototypes, gathering user feedback, and conducting usability testing to refine and improve functionality.
- Launch and market your productivity tool through digital platforms, social media channels, industry forums, and targeted advertising campaigns to reach your target audience, generate user sign-ups, and convert free trials into paid subscriptions, while providing excellent customer support and ongoing product updates.
- Monitor user engagement, retention, and feedback to identify opportunities for product enhancements, feature updates, and user experience improvements, iterating on your tool's development roadmap to align with user needs, market trends, and competitive dynamics.

52. Invest in Rental Properties in Tourist Destinations:

Investing in rental properties in tourist destinations involves acquiring residential or vacation rental properties located in popular tourist destinations, such as beachfront resorts, mountain retreats, or cultural landmarks, to generate rental income, capital appreciation, and diversification benefits from the hospitality industry.

Case Study:

David Johnson invested in vacation rental properties in a popular ski resort town, targeting seasonal tourists and outdoor enthusiasts seeking accommodations near ski slopes and recreational amenities. By offering well-appointed rental homes, superior guest experiences, and strategic pricing strategies, David's properties achieved high occupancy rates, favorable rental yields, and appreciation potential in a thriving tourist market.

Getting Started:

- Research and select tourist destinations with strong demand drivers, attractive amenities, and favorable market dynamics for vacation rentals, considering factors such as proximity to attractions, accessibility, tourism infrastructure, and rental regulations.
- Assess the financial feasibility and investment potential of rental properties in target tourist destinations, analyzing factors such as property prices, rental yields, occupancy rates, operating expenses, property management options, and potential risks associated with seasonal fluctuations or economic downturns.
- Identify suitable rental properties that meet investment criteria, such as location, property type, size, condition, rental potential, and budget constraints, conducting due diligence, property inspections, and financial analysis to

evaluate investment opportunities and negotiate favorable purchase terms.

- Develop a rental property management strategy, including marketing, pricing, guest services, maintenance, and guest communication, to attract bookings, provide memorable guest experiences, and maximize rental income while minimizing vacancies, property damage, and operational expenses.

- Implement a comprehensive asset management plan for rental properties, including regular maintenance, property upgrades, insurance coverage, and financial reporting, to preserve property value, enhance guest satisfaction, and optimize investment returns over the long term.

53. Start a Successful Personal Branding Agency:

Starting a successful personal branding agency involves helping individuals, professionals, entrepreneurs, or influencers build and promote their personal brand identities, online presence, and reputation across digital platforms, leveraging branding strategies, content marketing, and creative services to enhance visibility, credibility, and influence.

Case Study:

Rebecca Smith founded a personal branding agency specializing in executive branding and thought leadership development for C-suite executives and industry experts. By offering strategic brand positioning, content creation, media relations, and digital marketing services, Rebecca's agency helped clients differentiate themselves, establish authority, and attract opportunities for speaking engagements, partnerships, and career advancement.

Getting Started:

- Define your agency's niche, target market, and unique value proposition within the personal branding industry, such as executive branding, influencer branding, career coaching, or online reputation management, based on your expertise, network, and market demand.
- Develop a range of personalized branding services, packages, and offerings tailored to clients' goals, preferences, and budget, including brand strategy development, content creation, social media management, website design, and public relations campaigns, to address diverse client needs and objectives.
- Build a team of branding specialists, content creators, designers, and digital marketers with expertise in personal branding, storytelling, visual identity, and online engagement, ensuring collaboration, creativity, and professionalism in delivering client projects and campaigns.
- Establish partnerships and collaborations with industry influencers, media outlets, event organizers, and professional networks to expand your agency's reach, visibility, and client referrals, while showcasing success stories, client testimonials, and case studies to demonstrate your agency's value and impact.
- Implement scalable systems, processes, and technology platforms to streamline agency operations, project management, client communications, and performance tracking, ensuring efficiency, quality control, and client

satisfaction in delivering branding services and campaigns.

54. Offer Specialized Event Management or Wedding Planning Services:

Offering specialized event management or wedding planning services involves planning, coordinating, and executing memorable events, celebrations, or ceremonies for individuals, couples, corporations, or organizations, providing personalized service, attention to detail, and creative solutions to meet clients' event objectives and preferences.

Case Study:

Jessica Taylor established an event management company specializing in luxury weddings and social events for discerning clients. By offering full-service event planning, design, and coordination services, Jessica's company created bespoke experiences, curated vendor partnerships, and orchestrated flawless celebrations that exceeded clients' expectations and garnered rave reviews, earning a reputation as a premier event planner in the industry.

Getting Started:

- Determine your area of specialization within the event management industry, such as weddings, corporate events, fundraisers, galas, or private celebrations, based on your interests, experience, and market demand, and define your unique value proposition and service offerings.

- Develop relationships and partnerships with trusted vendors, venues, suppliers, and service providers in your target market, including florists, caterers, photographers, musicians, decorators, and rental companies, to offer comprehensive event solutions and ensure quality, reliability, and professionalism in execution.
- Create customizable event planning packages, pricing structures, and service contracts tailored to different client budgets, preferences, and event requirements, providing transparency, flexibility, and clarity in your offerings and terms to attract clients and secure bookings.
- Invest in professional development, industry certifications, and ongoing training to enhance your event planning skills, knowledge of industry trends, best practices, and vendor resources, and stay updated on emerging technologies, event software, and marketing strategies to improve efficiency and effectiveness in event management.
- Market and promote your event planning services through targeted advertising, social media marketing, wedding expos, bridal publications, and networking events, showcasing your portfolio, testimonials, and success stories to attract clients, build credibility, and differentiate your brand in a competitive market.

55. Develop and Sell a Successful Online Therapy Platform:

Developing and selling a successful online therapy platform involves creating a digital platform or app that connects individuals seeking mental health support with licensed therapists or counselors, offering convenient, accessible, and confidential therapy sessions through video conferencing, messaging, or phone calls.

Case Study:

Michael Johnson launched an online therapy platform offering on-demand counseling services for individuals struggling with anxiety, depression, or relationship issues. By partnering with licensed therapists, implementing secure communication channels, and prioritizing user privacy and confidentiality, Michael's platform provided a safe and supportive environment for users to access therapy from the comfort of their homes, generating revenue through subscription plans and session fees.

Getting Started:

- Define your target audience and therapy focus areas within the mental health market, such as individual therapy, couples counseling, family therapy, or specialized interventions for specific issues or populations, based on user needs, market research, and regulatory considerations.
- Recruit licensed therapists or counselors with diverse expertise, credentials, and specialties to join your platform, ensuring compliance with licensing requirements, ethical standards, and professional regulations governing online therapy practice, and provide training, supervision, and support to therapists using your platform.
- Develop a user-friendly online platform or mobile app for therapy sessions, incorporating features for appointment scheduling, secure video calls, messaging,

progress tracking, and payment processing, while prioritizing usability, accessibility, and data security to enhance the user experience and build trust.
- Establish pricing plans, subscription models, or pay-per-session fees for therapy services, offering flexible options, insurance billing, and financial assistance programs to accommodate different user preferences, financial situations, and insurance coverage, while ensuring transparency, affordability, and value for clients.
- Market and promote your online therapy platform through digital channels, social media platforms, mental health forums, professional networks, and partnerships with employers, healthcare providers, and wellness organizations, highlighting the benefits of accessible, convenient, and confidential therapy services available on your platform.

56. Invest in Index Funds for Diversified Exposure to the Market:

Investing in index funds for diversified exposure to the market involves allocating capital to passively managed investment funds that track a broad market index, such as the S&P 500, NASDAQ, or Dow Jones Industrial Average, to achieve diversified exposure to a range of stocks or securities with low costs and minimal active management.

Case Study:

Sarah Smith invested in a diversified index fund that tracked the performance of the S&P 500, providing exposure to a diverse portfolio of large-cap U.S. stocks across various sectors and industries. By investing regularly over time and reinvesting dividends, Sarah benefited from broad market exposure, reduced volatility, and competitive long-term returns compared to actively managed funds or individual stock picking strategies.

Getting Started:

- Choose an appropriate index fund or exchange-traded fund (ETF) that aligns with your investment goals, risk tolerance, and time horizon, considering factors such as fund performance, expense ratios, tracking error, liquidity, and asset allocation strategy, and research reputable fund providers and financial institutions offering index funds.
- Open a brokerage account or investment platform that offers access to index funds, ETFs, or mutual funds with no or low trading fees, account minimums, and administrative costs, and consider tax-efficient investment accounts such as individual retirement accounts (IRAs) or 401(k) plans for long-term investing.
- Determine your desired asset allocation and investment strategy based on your financial goals, risk profile, and investment timeframe, considering factors such as diversification, asset class exposure, and rebalancing frequency to achieve optimal portfolio performance and risk management.
- Invest regularly and systematically in index funds through dollar-cost averaging or automatic investment plans, contributing a portion of your income or savings at regular intervals to take advantage of market fluctuations and benefit from long-term compounding returns, while

maintaining a disciplined and consistent approach to investing.
- Monitor your index fund investments periodically, reviewing portfolio performance, asset allocation, and market conditions, and make adjustments as needed to rebalance your portfolio, reallocate assets, or align your investment strategy with changing financial goals or market dynamics.

57. Start a Successful Influencer Marketing Agency:

Starting a successful influencer marketing agency involves connecting brands with influencers or content creators to create authentic, engaging, and effective marketing campaigns that leverage influencers' social media influence, audience reach, and credibility to promote products, services, or brand messages to target audiences.

Case Study:

Rachel Carter founded an influencer marketing agency specializing in lifestyle brands and social media influencers. By curating influencer partnerships, negotiating brand collaborations, and measuring campaign performance, Rachel's agency helped clients reach new audiences, drive engagement, and increase sales through influencer endorsements and sponsored content, delivering measurable ROI and brand visibility.

Getting Started:
- Identify your agency's niche, focus areas, and target clientele within the influencer marketing industry, such as

beauty, fashion, fitness, travel, or niche markets, based on your expertise, network, and market demand, and define your agency's unique value proposition and service offerings.

- Build a roster of diverse influencers, content creators, and social media personalities with authentic voices, engaged audiences, and relevant demographics or interests, conducting talent scouting, outreach, and relationship building to establish partnerships and collaborations.
- Develop customized influencer marketing strategies, campaign concepts, and content briefs for clients, aligning brand objectives, target audience demographics, and key performance indicators (KPIs) with influencer selection, content creation, and campaign execution, while ensuring transparency, authenticity, and compliance with advertising regulations.
- Provide end-to-end campaign management, including influencer coordination, content production, campaign tracking, performance analytics, and reporting, to optimize campaign effectiveness, maximize ROI, and deliver value for clients, while maintaining communication, feedback loops, and relationship management with clients and influencers.
- Expand your agency's reach, visibility, and client base through networking, industry events, thought leadership content, and digital marketing efforts, showcasing successful case studies, client testimonials, and campaign results to attract new clients, build credibility, and differentiate your agency in a competitive market.

58. Offer Specialized HR Consulting or Recruitment Services:

Offering specialized HR consulting or recruitment services involves providing expert advice, solutions, and support to businesses, organizations, or individuals in areas such as talent acquisition, human resources management, organizational development, and workforce planning, leveraging HR expertise, industry knowledge, and best practices to drive business success.

Case Study:

Mark Thompson established an HR consulting firm specializing in executive search and talent management for technology startups. By offering strategic recruitment, leadership development, and HR advisory services, Mark's firm helped startups attract top talent, build high-performing teams, and scale operations, contributing to growth, innovation, and competitive advantage in the technology sector.

Getting Started:

- Define your HR consulting niche, focus areas, and target clientele within the human resources industry, such as recruitment, talent development, employee relations, compliance, or organizational design, based on your expertise, network, and market demand, and articulate your unique value proposition and service offerings.
- Develop a range of HR consulting services, solutions, and deliverables tailored to client needs, business objectives, and industry requirements, including recruitment strategy development, job analysis, candidate sourcing, selection assessments, performance

management, HR policies, and compliance audits, to address diverse HR challenges and opportunities.
- Build relationships and partnerships with businesses, startups, non-profit organizations, and industry associations to understand their HR needs, challenges, and goals, and offer customized consulting solutions, workshops, training programs, or advisory services to support their talent acquisition, retention, and development strategies.
- Leverage technology, data analytics, and HR tools to enhance recruitment processes, streamline workflows, and improve decision-making, while staying informed about emerging trends, best practices, and regulatory changes in the HR field to provide informed advice, insights, and solutions to clients.
- Market and promote your HR consulting services through networking, referrals, thought leadership content, speaking engagements, and digital marketing efforts, showcasing your expertise, track record, and client success stories to attract new clients, build trust, and establish credibility as a trusted HR advisor and partner.

59. Develop and Sell a Successful Online Travel Booking Platform:

Developing and selling a successful online travel booking platform involves creating a user-friendly website or mobile app that enables travelers to search, compare, and book flights, accommodations, transportation, activities, and travel packages, providing convenience, choice, and value-added services for travelers worldwide.

Case Study:

Laura Martinez launched an online travel booking platform offering curated travel experiences and personalized recommendations for adventurous travelers. By partnering with airlines, hotels, tour operators, and local vendors, Laura's platform provided seamless booking experiences, exclusive deals, and expert travel advice, attracting a loyal user base and generating revenue through commissions and booking fees.

Getting Started:

- Identify your target audience, travel niche, and competitive positioning within the online travel industry, such as budget travel, luxury travel, adventure travel, family vacations, or niche markets, based on market research, user preferences, and industry trends.
- Develop a user-friendly online platform or mobile app with intuitive search functionality, comprehensive travel listings, secure payment processing, and responsive customer support, focusing on usability, speed, reliability, and accessibility to enhance the user experience and drive conversions.
- Establish partnerships and collaborations with travel suppliers, including airlines, hotels, car rental companies, tour operators, activity providers, and destination management organizations, to access inventory, negotiate favorable rates, and offer competitive pricing, while ensuring quality, reliability, and customer satisfaction.

- Implement marketing and promotional strategies to attract travelers, including search engine optimization (SEO), content marketing, social media advertising, email campaigns, affiliate partnerships, and referral programs, to increase website traffic, engagement, and bookings, while leveraging user reviews, testimonials, and endorsements to build trust and credibility.
- Monitor and analyze website performance, booking trends, user feedback, and competitive landscape to identify opportunities for optimization, innovation, and expansion, while staying informed about emerging technologies, industry developments, and traveler preferences to adapt your platform and services accordingly.

60. Invest in Real Estate Investment Trusts (REITs) for Passive Income:

Investing in Real Estate Investment Trusts (REITs) for passive income involves purchasing shares or units in publicly traded or private REITs, which own, operate, or finance income-generating real estate properties such as residential apartments, commercial buildings, shopping malls, or industrial facilities, to receive regular dividends and potential capital appreciation.

Case Study:

James Johnson invested in a diversified portfolio of REITs representing various property sectors, including residential, retail, office, and healthcare real estate. By allocating capital to REITs with stable cash flows, strong management teams, and diversified property portfolios, James generated passive income through quarterly dividends, while benefiting from potential long-term growth and inflation hedging properties of real estate investments.

Getting Started:

- Research and evaluate different types of REITs available in the market, including equity REITs, mortgage REITs, and hybrid REITs, as well as publicly traded, private, or exchange-traded REITs, considering factors such as property types, geographic locations, risk profiles, dividend yields, and investment strategies.
- Determine your investment goals, risk tolerance, and income needs, and select REITs that align with your financial objectives, portfolio diversification goals, and investment timeframe, while assessing liquidity, tax implications, and potential risks associated with REIT investments.
- Open a brokerage account or investment platform that offers access to REITs, mutual funds, or ETFs specializing in real estate securities, and consider tax-advantaged investment accounts such as individual retirement accounts (IRAs) or 401(k) plans for tax-efficient investing and retirement planning.
- Allocate a portion of your investment portfolio to REITs based on your asset allocation strategy, investment horizon, and income requirements, and monitor performance, dividend distributions, and market conditions to rebalance your portfolio, reinvest dividends, or adjust your investment strategy as needed to achieve your financial goals.

- Consult with a financial advisor or investment professional to assess your suitability for REIT investments, understand potential risks and rewards, and develop a personalized investment plan that aligns with your overall financial situation, objectives, and risk profile.

61. **Start a Successful Digital Marketing Agency:**

Starting a successful digital marketing agency involves providing comprehensive marketing services to businesses, brands, or individuals, including website design, search engine optimization (SEO), content marketing, social media management, email marketing, pay-per-click (PPC) advertising, and analytics, to improve online visibility, generate leads, and drive conversions.

Case Study:

Emily Roberts founded a digital marketing agency specializing in small businesses and startups. By offering tailored digital marketing solutions, personalized strategies, and measurable results, Emily's agency helped clients enhance their online presence, attract targeted traffic, and achieve business growth through effective online marketing campaigns and strategies.

Getting Started:

- Define your agency's niche, target market, and unique value proposition within the digital marketing industry, such as industry specialization, service focus, or

geographic location, based on your expertise, experience, and market demand.
- Develop a range of digital marketing services, packages, and solutions tailored to client needs, objectives, and budget constraints, including website development, SEO audits, content creation, social media management, email campaigns, and digital advertising, to address diverse marketing challenges and goals.
- Build a team of skilled professionals, including marketers, designers, developers, writers, and analysts, with expertise in different areas of digital marketing, ensuring collaboration, creativity, and professionalism in delivering client projects and campaigns.
- Establish partnerships and collaborations with complementary service providers, such as web developers, graphic designers, copywriters, and marketing technology platforms, to offer integrated solutions, expand service offerings, and deliver comprehensive marketing solutions to clients.
- Implement scalable systems, processes, and technology platforms to streamline agency operations, project management, client communications, and performance tracking, ensuring efficiency, quality control, and client satisfaction in delivering digital marketing services and campaigns.

62. Offer Specialized Executive Coaching or Leadership Development Programs:

Offering specialized executive coaching or leadership development programs involves providing personalized coaching, mentoring, and training to executives, leaders, managers, or entrepreneurs to enhance their leadership skills, emotional intelligence, decision-making abilities, and career advancement prospects.

Case Study:

David Wilson launched an executive coaching firm specializing in leadership development for C-suite executives. By offering tailored coaching sessions, leadership assessments, and skill-building workshops, David helped executives overcome challenges, unlock their potential, and achieve greater success and fulfillment in their professional and personal lives.

Getting Started:

- Define your coaching niche, target audience, and coaching approach within the executive coaching industry, such as leadership development, career transitions, performance coaching, or work-life balance, based on your expertise, credentials, and market demand.
- Develop a range of coaching programs, packages, and interventions tailored to client needs, objectives, and leadership competencies, including one-on-one coaching sessions, group workshops, leadership assessments, and development plans, to address specific leadership challenges and goals.
- Obtain relevant coaching certifications, credentials, or accreditations from recognized coaching organizations or professional bodies to establish credibility, demonstrate expertise, and adhere to ethical standards and best practices in coaching, while continuing professional

development to stay updated on coaching methodologies, research, and trends.
- Market and promote your coaching services through networking, referrals, speaking engagements, thought leadership content, and digital marketing efforts, targeting executives, HR professionals, leadership development programs, and corporate clients, while showcasing client testimonials, success stories, and case studies to illustrate the impact and value of your coaching services.
- Build strategic partnerships and collaborations with organizations, universities, training providers, and professional networks to offer executive coaching as part of leadership development programs, talent management initiatives, or career advancement pathways, while leveraging your expertise, reputation, and network to attract clients and expand your coaching practice.

63. Develop and Sell a Successful Online Language Learning Platform:

Developing and selling a successful online language learning platform involves creating an interactive and engaging digital platform or app that offers language courses, lessons, exercises, and practice opportunities for learners of all levels, catering to diverse learning styles, preferences, and language proficiency goals.

Case Study:

Maria Garcia launched an online language learning platform offering courses in Spanish, French, and German. By combining structured lessons, interactive exercises, multimedia content, and personalized feedback, Maria's platform provided effective and enjoyable language learning experiences for students worldwide, generating revenue through course subscriptions, premium features, and language proficiency certifications.

Getting Started:

- Choose the target language(s) and target audience for your online language learning platform, considering factors such as language demand, learner demographics, competition, and market trends, and conduct market research to identify niche opportunities, learner preferences, and unmet needs.
- Develop a comprehensive curriculum and learning pathway for each language offered on your platform, including beginner, intermediate, and advanced levels, grammar instruction, vocabulary building, speaking practice, listening comprehension, and cultural insights, while integrating multimedia resources, interactive exercises, and gamification elements to enhance engagement and retention.
- Build a user-friendly and intuitive online platform or mobile app with features for course navigation, progress tracking, interactive lessons, speaking exercises, feedback mechanisms, and community engagement, prioritizing accessibility, responsiveness, and user experience to accommodate learners of all ages and proficiency levels.
- Recruit qualified language instructors or native speakers to create course content, deliver live or recorded lessons, provide feedback and support, and facilitate language practice sessions, ensuring expertise, professionalism,

and cultural authenticity in language instruction and communication.
- Implement marketing and promotion strategies to attract language learners, including search engine optimization (SEO), content marketing, social media advertising, influencer partnerships, and affiliate programs, while leveraging testimonials, student success stories, and language proficiency achievements to demonstrate the effectiveness and value of your language learning platform.

64. Invest in Peer-to-Peer Lending Platforms for High Returns:

Investing in peer-to-peer (P2P) lending platforms for high returns involves allocating capital to online lending platforms that connect borrowers with individual or institutional investors seeking attractive fixed-income investments, enabling investors to earn competitive interest rates by lending money directly to borrowers.

Case Study:

Jonathan Smith invested in peer-to-peer lending platforms offering personal loans to creditworthy borrowers. By diversifying his investment portfolio across multiple P2P lending platforms, loan grades, and borrower profiles, Jonathan earned consistent returns averaging 7% to 10% annually, outperforming traditional fixed-income investments such as savings accounts or bonds.

Getting Started:

- Research and evaluate different peer-to-peer lending platforms available in the market, considering factors such as loan types, borrower profiles, interest rates, loan terms, default rates, platform fees, investor protection measures, and regulatory compliance, and choose platforms that align with your risk tolerance, investment goals, and liquidity needs.
- Open an investor account or investment fund on your chosen P2P lending platforms, complete account verification, and transfer funds to your investment account, while adhering to platform requirements, investor eligibility criteria, and anti-money laundering (AML) regulations.
- Diversify your investment portfolio across multiple loans, loan grades, and borrower profiles to mitigate credit risk and increase investment returns, allocating capital strategically based on loan performance, borrower creditworthiness, and interest rate considerations, while reinvesting principal and interest payments to compound your returns over time.
- Monitor loan performance, borrower repayments, and platform updates regularly, using investment dashboards, performance metrics, and risk indicators provided by P2P lending platforms to track portfolio performance, assess credit risk, and make informed investment decisions, while staying informed about changes in market conditions, regulatory developments, and platform policies that may affect your investment strategy.
- Rebalance your P2P lending portfolio periodically, adjusting investment allocations, reinvestment settings, or withdrawal strategies based on changing market

conditions, investment goals, and risk preferences, while maintaining a disciplined and diversified approach to P2P lending investing to achieve consistent returns and manage investment risk effectively.

65. Start a Successful Subscription Box Service:

Starting a successful subscription box service involves curating, packaging, and delivering themed boxes of products or experiences to subscribers on a recurring basis, offering convenience, discovery, and value-added offerings tailored to specific interests, hobbies, lifestyles, or niche markets.

Case Study:

Sarah Thompson launched a subscription box service specializing in eco-friendly household products and sustainable living essentials. By sourcing high-quality, ethically sourced products, designing eco-friendly packaging, and delivering personalized customer experiences, Sarah's subscription box service attracted environmentally conscious consumers, generating recurring revenue through monthly subscriptions and add-on purchases.

Getting Started:

- Identify a niche or target market for your subscription box service, such as beauty, fitness, food, wellness, pets, hobbies, or niche interests, based on market research, consumer preferences, and industry trends, and define your unique selling proposition (USP) and value proposition to differentiate your offering from competitors.

- Source or create a selection of products, samples, or experiences to include in your subscription boxes, considering factors such as product quality, brand reputation, consumer demand, pricing, and packaging suitability, while negotiating wholesale discounts, bulk orders, or exclusive partnerships with suppliers and vendors.
- Design and customize your subscription box packaging, branding, and marketing materials to reflect your brand identity, theme, and value proposition, incorporating eye-catching graphics, personalized messages, and eco-friendly materials to enhance unboxing experiences and delight subscribers.
- Launch and promote your subscription box service through various channels, including social media, email marketing, influencer collaborations, affiliate partnerships, and promotional events, offering incentives, discounts, or referral programs to attract new subscribers and retain existing customers, while providing exceptional customer service, feedback mechanisms, and subscription flexibility to optimize subscriber satisfaction and retention.
- Analyze subscriber feedback, engagement metrics, and sales data to iterate and improve your subscription box offerings, product selection, packaging design, pricing strategy, and customer experience, while staying responsive to market trends, consumer preferences, and competitive dynamics to sustain growth and profitability in the subscription box industry.

66. Offer Specialized Data Analysis or Business Intelligence Services:

Offering specialized data analysis or business intelligence services involves providing organizations with insights, analytics, and actionable recommendations derived from data-driven analysis of business operations, market trends, customer behavior, and performance metrics, enabling informed decision-making and strategic planning.

Case Study:

John Davis founded a data analytics consultancy specializing in retail analytics and consumer behavior analysis. By leveraging advanced analytics tools, machine learning algorithms, and predictive modeling techniques, John's consultancy helped retailers optimize pricing strategies, inventory management, and marketing campaigns, driving revenue growth and competitive advantage in the retail sector.

Getting Started:

- Identify your target market, industry focus, and specialized expertise within the data analytics or business intelligence field, such as financial services, healthcare, e-commerce, marketing, or supply chain management, based on your skills, experience, and market demand, and define your unique value proposition and service offerings.
- Develop a range of data analysis services, solutions, and methodologies tailored to client needs, business objectives, and industry challenges, including data visualization, predictive analytics, trend analysis, customer segmentation, risk assessment, and

performance benchmarking, to deliver actionable insights and recommendations that drive business outcomes.

- Invest in data analytics tools, software platforms, and technologies that support data integration, cleansing, modeling, and visualization, while staying abreast of emerging technologies, industry trends, and best practices in data analytics, machine learning, artificial intelligence, and business intelligence to enhance your analytical capabilities and service offerings.

- Build relationships and partnerships with businesses, organizations, and industry associations to understand their data analytics needs, challenges, and goals, and offer customized consulting services, workshops, training programs, or analytics-as-a-service (AaaS) solutions to support their data-driven decision-making, performance optimization, and innovation initiatives.

- Market and promote your data analysis services through thought leadership content, case studies, industry events, and digital marketing efforts, showcasing your expertise, track record, and client success stories to attract new clients, build trust, and establish credibility as a trusted data analytics advisor and partner.

67. Develop and Sell a Successful Online Cooking or Recipe Platform:

Developing and selling a successful online cooking or recipe platform involves creating a digital platform or website that offers a diverse collection of recipes, cooking tutorials, meal planning tools, and culinary content to food enthusiasts, home cooks, and aspiring chefs, providing inspiration, guidance, and resources for cooking at home.

Case Study:

Rachel Smith launched an online cooking platform featuring easy-to-follow recipes, cooking videos, and meal prep guides. By collaborating with chefs, nutritionists, and food bloggers, Rachel's platform attracted a large audience of food lovers, generating revenue through advertising, sponsored content, affiliate partnerships, and premium membership subscriptions.

Getting Started:

- Define your target audience, culinary niche, and content focus for your online cooking platform, such as healthy recipes, international cuisine, plant-based cooking, gourmet dishes, or budget-friendly meals, based on market research, audience preferences, and culinary trends.
- Create and curate a diverse collection of high-quality recipes, cooking tutorials, culinary tips, and kitchen hacks to populate your platform, leveraging user-generated content, professional chefs, food influencers, and culinary experts to enrich your content library and engage your audience.
- Design and optimize your online cooking platform for user experience, accessibility, and mobile responsiveness, incorporating features for recipe search, filtering, rating, and commenting, as well as meal planning tools, shopping lists, and cooking guides to enhance user engagement and retention.
- Monetize your online cooking platform through various revenue streams, including display advertising, sponsored

- content partnerships, affiliate marketing programs, premium membership subscriptions, e-commerce sales of cooking equipment or ingredients, and branded merchandise, while balancing user experience, content quality, and monetization strategies to maximize revenue and user satisfaction.
- Promote and grow your online cooking platform through content marketing, social media outreach, influencer collaborations, email newsletters, cooking contests, and community engagement initiatives, while leveraging analytics, user feedback, and performance metrics to optimize content strategy, audience engagement, and platform growth over time.

68. Invest in High-Quality Dividend-Paying Bonds:

Investing in high-quality dividend-paying bonds involves allocating capital to fixed-income securities issued by governments, municipalities, corporations, or agencies, which offer regular interest payments (dividends) and return of principal upon maturity, providing stable income, capital preservation, and portfolio diversification benefits.

Case Study:

Sarah Johnson invested in a diversified portfolio of high-quality municipal bonds offering tax-exempt income and competitive yields. By selecting bonds with strong credit ratings, predictable cash flows, and favorable interest rates, Sarah generated consistent income and capital preservation in her investment portfolio, while managing risk through asset allocation and credit analysis.

Getting Started:

- Understand the characteristics and risks of bonds, including credit risk, interest rate risk, inflation risk, liquidity risk, and default risk, and assess your investment objectives, risk tolerance, and income needs to determine the appropriate allocation to bonds within your investment portfolio.
- Research and evaluate different types of bonds available in the market, including government bonds, municipal bonds, corporate bonds, agency bonds, and treasury inflation-protected securities (TIPS), considering factors such as credit quality, yield-to-maturity, maturity date, tax treatment, and liquidity, and choose bonds that align with your investment goals and risk preferences.
- Select high-quality bonds issued by reputable issuers with strong credit ratings, stable cash flows, and favorable yield spreads relative to benchmark interest rates, while diversifying across different issuers, sectors, maturities, and geographic regions to reduce concentration risk and enhance portfolio resilience.
- Build a bond portfolio with a laddered maturity structure or diversified duration exposure to manage interest rate risk and reinvestment risk effectively, while incorporating tax-efficient bond strategies such as municipal bonds for taxable investors or tax-exempt bonds for tax-sensitive investors to optimize after-tax returns and minimize tax liabilities.
- Monitor and rebalance your bond portfolio periodically, adjusting bond holdings, maturities, and duration targets based on changing market conditions, interest rate expectations, credit outlook, and economic indicators,

while staying informed about regulatory changes, issuer developments, and credit rating updates that may impact bond prices and portfolio performance.

69. Start a Successful Influencer Management Agency:

Starting a successful influencer management agency involves representing and collaborating with social media influencers, content creators, and digital personalities to connect them with brands, businesses, and marketing campaigns, facilitating partnerships, negotiations, and brand collaborations for mutual benefit.

Case Study:

Jessica Lee founded an influencer management agency specializing in lifestyle influencers and fashion bloggers. By building strong relationships with influencers, brands, and agencies, Jessica's agency facilitated successful brand partnerships, sponsored content collaborations, and influencer marketing campaigns, generating revenue through management fees, commissions, and brand partnerships.

Getting Started:

- Define your agency's niche, focus, and specialization within the influencer marketing industry, such as lifestyle, fashion, beauty, fitness, travel, or niche interests, based on market research, industry trends, and your network of influencers and brands.
- Build a roster of talented and diverse influencers across different social media platforms, including Instagram,

YouTube, TikTok, Facebook, Twitter, and Pinterest, by scouting, recruiting, and vetting influencers based on audience demographics, engagement metrics, content quality, and brand alignment.
- Develop comprehensive influencer management services, including talent representation, brand partnerships, campaign management, content creation, contract negotiation, and performance tracking, to provide value-added services and support to influencers and brands throughout the collaboration process.
- Forge partnerships and collaborations with brands, agencies, PR firms, and marketing platforms to identify collaboration opportunities, secure sponsorship deals, and execute influencer marketing campaigns that align with client objectives, target audience, and brand values, while maximizing reach, engagement, and ROI.
- Market and promote your influencer management agency through networking events, industry conferences, social media channels, influencer showcases, and agency directories, while leveraging success stories, case studies, and testimonials to showcase your agency's track record, expertise, and value proposition to potential clients and influencers.

70. Offer Specialized HR Consulting or Recruitment Services:

Offering specialized HR consulting or recruitment services involves providing strategic HR solutions, talent acquisition services, and workforce management expertise to businesses, organizations, and HR departments, helping them attract, retain, and develop top talent while optimizing HR processes and practices.

Case Study:

Michael Johnson launched an HR consulting firm specializing in talent acquisition and workforce planning. By offering tailored HR solutions, recruitment strategies, and talent management programs, Michael's firm helped clients improve employee retention, streamline hiring processes, and build high-performing teams, generating revenue through consulting fees and project-based engagements.

Getting Started:

- Identify your HR consulting niche, focus area, and service offerings within the HR industry, such as recruitment, talent management, employee relations, organizational development, compensation and benefits, HR technology, or compliance, based on your expertise, credentials, and market demand.
- Develop a range of HR consulting services, solutions, and methodologies tailored to client needs, business objectives, and HR challenges, including HR audits, policy development, performance management, leadership training, diversity and inclusion initiatives, and HR technology implementation, to address specific HR issues and goals.
- Build relationships and partnerships with businesses, HR departments, industry associations, and professional networks to understand their HR needs, challenges, and priorities, and offer customized consulting services, workshops, training programs, or HR-as-a-service (HRaaS) solutions to support their HR transformation,

talent acquisition, and organizational development initiatives.

- Market and promote your HR consulting services through thought leadership content, industry events, speaking engagements, webinars, and digital marketing efforts, positioning yourself as a trusted advisor and subject matter expert in HR best practices, trends, and innovations, while leveraging client testimonials, success stories, and case studies to demonstrate the impact and value of your consulting services.

71. Develop and Sell a Successful Online Music Streaming Platform:

Developing and selling a successful online music streaming platform involves creating a digital platform or app that offers a vast catalog of music content, personalized playlists, curated recommendations, and seamless streaming experiences for users, while providing revenue opportunities for artists, labels, and content creators.

Case Study:

David Brown founded an online music streaming platform that focused on independent artists and emerging genres. By offering a diverse selection of music, promoting new talent, and providing fair compensation to artists through revenue-sharing models, David's platform attracted a loyal user base and generated revenue through subscription fees, advertising, and merchandise sales.

Getting Started:

- Identify your target audience, music genres, and value proposition for your online music streaming platform, considering factors such as user preferences, competition, licensing requirements, and market trends, and define your unique selling points to differentiate your platform in the crowded streaming market.
- Secure licensing agreements with music labels, publishers, and rights holders to access a comprehensive catalog of music content, including popular hits, niche genres, independent artists, and exclusive releases, while complying with copyright laws, royalty payments, and digital rights management (DRM) protocols.
- Design and develop a user-friendly and feature-rich music streaming platform or mobile app with intuitive navigation, personalized recommendations, social sharing features, offline playback options, and interactive community features to enhance user engagement and retention.
- Implement monetization strategies such as subscription-based plans, ad-supported free tiers, premium features, merchandise sales, and concert ticket promotions to generate revenue from your music streaming platform, while balancing user experience, content quality, and revenue generation goals.
- Market and promote your online music streaming platform through digital marketing campaigns, social media engagement, influencer partnerships, music festivals, and artist collaborations, while leveraging user-generated content, playlist curation, and community engagement to foster a vibrant and loyal user community.

72. Invest in Angel Investing or Startup Incubators:

Investing in angel investing or startup incubators involves providing early-stage funding, mentorship, and support to promising startups, entrepreneurs, and innovators in exchange for equity ownership, helping them grow, scale, and succeed in competitive markets.

Case Study:

Sarah Johnson became an angel investor and joined a startup incubator program focused on technology startups. By investing in innovative ventures, providing strategic guidance, and leveraging her industry connections, Sarah supported startups in raising capital, developing products, and entering new markets, while diversifying her investment portfolio and earning returns through successful exits and acquisitions.

Getting Started:

- Educate yourself about the angel investing process, investment criteria, risk factors, and due diligence procedures involved in evaluating startup opportunities, and assess your investment objectives, risk tolerance, and investment horizon to align with your angel investing strategy.
- Join angel investor networks, investment syndicates, or startup accelerators to gain access to deal flow, investment opportunities, and co-investment opportunities with other angel investors, while leveraging mentorship, networking events, and resources offered by the investor community.
- Conduct thorough due diligence on potential startup investments, assessing factors such as market potential,

product-market fit, competitive landscape, team capabilities, financial projections, and exit strategies, and negotiate investment terms, valuation, and shareholder agreements to protect your interests and maximize potential returns.

- Provide value-added support and mentorship to portfolio startups, leveraging your industry expertise, networks, and resources to help founders overcome challenges, validate business models, access talent and capital, and accelerate growth, while actively participating in board meetings, strategic decision-making, and fundraising efforts.

- Monitor and manage your angel investment portfolio actively, tracking key performance indicators, milestones, and financial metrics for each startup, while staying engaged with founders, advisors, and co-investors to address issues, seize opportunities, and navigate challenges throughout the startup lifecycle, with a focus on maximizing investor value and achieving successful exits.

73. Start a Successful Digital Advertising Agency:

Starting a successful digital advertising agency involves providing comprehensive advertising and marketing services across digital channels, including search engines, social media platforms, display networks, and content publishers, to help businesses reach and engage their target audiences effectively.

Case Study:

Emily White launched a digital advertising agency specializing in performance marketing and conversion optimization. By leveraging data-driven insights, creative strategies, and advanced ad tech solutions, Emily's agency helped clients increase brand visibility, drive website traffic, and generate qualified leads, while optimizing advertising spend and maximizing ROI across digital campaigns.

Getting Started:

- Define your digital advertising agency's niche, specialization, and service offerings within the digital marketing landscape, such as paid search advertising, social media marketing, display advertising, programmatic advertising, influencer marketing, content marketing, or email marketing, based on your expertise, industry trends, and client demand.
- Build a team of digital marketing specialists, including PPC experts, social media managers, content creators, data analysts, and account managers, with diverse skills, experience, and certifications in digital advertising platforms, tools, and technologies, to deliver comprehensive and integrated solutions to clients.
- Develop strategic partnerships and collaborations with technology providers, ad networks, media publishers, and marketing platforms to access cutting-edge advertising technologies, data analytics tools, audience targeting capabilities, and advertising inventory, while staying informed about industry trends, algorithm updates, and best practices in digital advertising.
- Customize digital advertising solutions and campaigns for each client based on their business goals, target audience, competitive landscape, and budget constraints,

leveraging audience segmentation, ad creative optimization, A/B testing, conversion tracking, and performance analytics to drive measurable results and continuous improvement.

- Market and promote your digital advertising agency through thought leadership content, case studies, client testimonials, industry awards, and networking events, showcasing your agency's expertise, track record, and value proposition to attract new clients, build trust, and establish long-term partnerships in the digital advertising industry.

74. Offer Specialized Healthcare Consulting or Telemedicine Services:

Offering specialized healthcare consulting or telemedicine services involves providing strategic advisory, operational support, and technology solutions to healthcare organizations, providers, and stakeholders, to optimize patient care delivery, improve clinical outcomes, and enhance healthcare efficiency and effectiveness.

Case Study:

Dr. James Smith founded a healthcare consulting firm specializing in telemedicine implementation and remote patient monitoring. By assisting healthcare providers in adopting telehealth technologies, integrating virtual care platforms, and redesigning care delivery models, Dr. Smith's firm improved access to healthcare services, reduced healthcare disparities, and enhanced patient engagement and satisfaction.

Getting Started:

- Identify your healthcare consulting niche, focus area, and service offerings within the healthcare industry, such as telemedicine, health IT, population health management, revenue cycle management, healthcare analytics, regulatory compliance, or value-based care, based on your expertise, credentials, and market demand.
- Build a team of healthcare consultants, clinicians, IT specialists, and project managers with diverse backgrounds and expertise in healthcare delivery, technology implementation, change management, and healthcare policy, to provide comprehensive consulting services and solutions to clients across the healthcare continuum.
- Develop customized healthcare consulting services and solutions tailored to client needs, organizational priorities, and healthcare challenges, including telemedicine strategy development, EHR optimization, interoperability planning, clinical workflow redesign, telehealth reimbursement optimization, regulatory compliance audits, cybersecurity assessments, and patient engagement strategies, to address specific healthcare issues and achieve organizational goals.
- Forge strategic partnerships and alliances with healthcare providers, hospitals, clinics, insurers, technology vendors, and industry associations to leverage expertise, resources, and networks, and collaborate on consulting projects, joint ventures, and business development opportunities in the healthcare market.
- Implement healthcare consulting projects and initiatives with a focus on collaboration, stakeholder engagement,

and change management, involving key stakeholders, clinicians, administrators, and IT teams in the planning, execution, and evaluation of consulting recommendations and solutions, while ensuring alignment with organizational goals, quality standards, and regulatory requirements.
- Measure and monitor the impact of healthcare consulting interventions, using performance metrics, key performance indicators (KPIs), and outcome measures to assess progress, evaluate effectiveness, and drive continuous improvement in healthcare delivery, patient outcomes, and financial performance, while providing ongoing support, training, and knowledge transfer to empower clients and sustain positive changes over time.

75. Develop and Sell a Successful Online Art Marketplace:

Developing and selling a successful online art marketplace involves creating a digital platform or website that connects artists, collectors, galleries, and art enthusiasts, providing a curated selection of artworks, personalized recommendations, and seamless transactions for buying and selling art online.

Case Study:

Julia Roberts launched an online art marketplace showcasing emerging artists and contemporary artwork. By offering a user-friendly platform, promoting artist profiles, and facilitating art sales and commissions, Julia's marketplace attracted a global audience of art lovers, generated revenue through transaction fees and premium memberships, and supported emerging talent in the art community.

Getting Started:

- Define your online art marketplace's mission, vision, and value proposition, focusing on aspects such as artist empowerment, art accessibility, community engagement, or art curation, to differentiate your platform and attract artists, collectors, and art enthusiasts to your marketplace.
- Curate a diverse and high-quality selection of artworks across different styles, mediums, and price points, partnering with artists, galleries, art dealers, and curators to source original artwork, limited editions, prints, and digital art for your online marketplace, while ensuring authenticity, quality, and copyright compliance.
- Develop an intuitive and visually appealing online platform or mobile app for your art marketplace, featuring artist profiles, artwork galleries, search filters, virtual exhibitions, bidding options, secure payment processing, and shipping logistics, to enhance the art browsing, discovery, and purchasing experience for users.
- Implement marketing and promotion strategies to attract artists and collectors to your online art marketplace, including social media campaigns, email newsletters, influencer partnerships, art fairs, and gallery events, while fostering a sense of community, trust, and transparency through artist interviews, collector testimonials, and educational content.
- Monetize your online art marketplace through various revenue streams, such as transaction fees, listing fees, membership subscriptions, premium features, art

appraisals, and commission-based sales, while reinvesting in artist support, platform development, and marketing initiatives to grow your marketplace and expand its reach in the global art market.

76. Invest in Rental Properties for Student Housing:

Investing in rental properties for student housing involves acquiring residential properties near colleges and universities, leasing them to student tenants, and generating rental income and capital appreciation from student housing investments.

Case Study:

John Taylor invested in rental properties located in college towns and student-friendly neighborhoods. By purchasing single-family homes, condominiums, or multi-unit apartment buildings near campus, John rented out the properties to students, earning steady rental income and benefiting from high occupancy rates, consistent demand, and long-term appreciation potential in student housing markets.

Getting Started:

- Research and identify college towns and university cities with strong student populations, reputable academic institutions, and robust rental markets, considering factors such as enrollment trends, housing demand, student demographics, and local economic indicators, to target viable investment opportunities.
- Evaluate potential rental properties for student housing based on criteria such as location, proximity to campus, neighborhood amenities, property condition, rental yield,

cash flow potential, and investment affordability, conducting property inspections, financial analysis, and due diligence to assess investment viability and risks.
- Purchase rental properties for student housing through various financing options, including conventional mortgages, FHA loans, portfolio loans, or private financing, leveraging equity, down payments, or investment partnerships to acquire properties with favorable terms, financing rates, and investment returns.
- Renovate, furnish, and prepare rental properties for student occupancy, addressing maintenance issues, safety concerns, and amenities desired by student tenants, such as high-speed internet, laundry facilities, parking spaces, communal areas, and proximity to campus amenities and transportation options, to attract and retain tenants.
- Manage rental properties for student housing effectively, handling tenant inquiries, lease agreements, rent collection, property maintenance, and tenant turnover, while providing responsive and proactive property management services to ensure tenant satisfaction, property upkeep, and compliance with rental regulations and university guidelines.

77. Start a Successful SEO (Search Engine Optimization) Agency:

Starting a successful SEO (Search Engine Optimization) agency involves providing expert SEO services, digital marketing strategies, and website optimization solutions to businesses, organizations, and brands, helping them improve their online visibility, organic search rankings, and website traffic.

Case Study:

Mark Johnson founded an SEO agency specializing in on-page optimization, link building, and content marketing strategies. By implementing tailored SEO strategies, conducting comprehensive website audits, and tracking key performance indicators, Mark's agency helped clients achieve higher search engine rankings, increased website traffic, and improved conversion rates, generating revenue through retainer fees and project-based contracts.

Getting Started:

- Define your SEO agency's niche, focus area, and service offerings within the SEO industry, such as technical SEO audits, keyword research, content optimization, link building, local SEO, e-commerce SEO, or enterprise SEO, based on your expertise, market demand, and client needs.
- Build a team of SEO specialists, digital marketers, content creators, web developers, and analytics experts with diverse skills and experience in search engine optimization, analytics tools, SEO software, and industry best practices, to deliver effective and results-driven SEO solutions to clients.
- Develop customized SEO strategies and campaigns for each client, based on their business goals, target audience, competitive landscape, and industry trends, leveraging data-driven insights, competitor analysis, keyword research, content optimization, technical SEO fixes, and

link-building tactics to improve organic search visibility and website performance.
- Implement SEO best practices and optimization techniques across clients' websites, including website architecture improvements, on-page SEO optimization, metadata optimization, internal linking strategies, mobile optimization, site speed optimization, and schema markup implementation, to enhance search engine crawling, indexing, and ranking.
- Provide ongoing SEO monitoring, reporting, and optimization services to clients, tracking key performance metrics, search engine rankings, organic traffic trends, and conversion rates, while adapting SEO strategies, tactics, and priorities based on algorithm updates, market changes, and client feedback, to ensure long-term success and continuous improvement in organic search performance.

78. Offer Specialized Sustainability Consulting or Green Energy Solutions:

Offering specialized sustainability consulting or green energy solutions involves providing advisory services, renewable energy solutions, and sustainability strategies to businesses, organizations, governments, and communities, to promote environmental stewardship, resource conservation, and sustainable development.

Case Study:

Rachel Adams established a sustainability consulting firm focusing on renewable energy projects and green building initiatives. By conducting energy audits, implementing solar installations, and advising clients on sustainability practices, Rachel's firm helped businesses reduce carbon emissions, lower energy costs, and achieve LEED certification, generating revenue through consulting fees and project-based contracts.

Getting Started:

- Identify your sustainability consulting niche, focus area, and service offerings within the sustainability industry, such as renewable energy, energy efficiency, waste management, green building, water conservation, carbon offsetting, sustainable supply chains, or corporate social responsibility (CSR), based on your expertise, passion, and market demand.
- Build a team of sustainability experts, engineers, environmental scientists, LEED professionals, and project managers with specialized knowledge and experience in sustainability consulting, green energy technologies, regulatory compliance, and environmental impact assessment, to deliver innovative and impactful solutions to clients.
- Develop customized sustainability strategies and solutions for clients, considering their sustainability goals, operational challenges, industry standards, and regulatory requirements, and offering a range of services such as energy audits, sustainability assessments, green technology adoption, carbon footprint reduction, and sustainability reporting.
- Implement renewable energy projects, green building initiatives, and sustainability programs for clients, leveraging solar photovoltaic systems, wind turbines, energy-efficient technologies, smart building solutions,

water-saving measures, waste reduction strategies, and eco-friendly practices to achieve measurable environmental and economic benefits.
- Provide ongoing support, monitoring, and performance optimization for sustainability initiatives, tracking key performance indicators, environmental metrics, and cost savings, while educating and engaging stakeholders, employees, and communities in sustainable practices and initiatives, to foster a culture of environmental responsibility and long-term sustainability.

79. Develop and Sell a Successful Online Tutoring Platform:

Developing and selling a successful online tutoring platform involves creating a digital marketplace or platform that connects students with tutors, educators, and subject matter experts, offering personalized learning experiences, academic support, and tutoring services across various subjects and disciplines.

Case Study:

Laura Martinez launched an online tutoring platform specializing in STEM subjects and test preparation. By recruiting qualified tutors, providing interactive learning materials, and offering flexible scheduling options, Laura's platform helped students improve their grades, enhance their academic performance, and prepare for standardized tests, generating revenue through subscription fees and tutor commissions.

Getting Started:

- Define your online tutoring platform's target audience, educational focus, and value proposition, considering factors such as student demographics, academic needs, learning preferences, competition analysis, and market trends, to differentiate your platform and attract students and tutors.
- Build a network of qualified tutors, educators, and subject matter experts with expertise in various disciplines, educational levels, and teaching styles, recruiting tutors with relevant credentials, teaching experience, background checks, and subject proficiency, to deliver high-quality tutoring services to students.
- Develop an intuitive and user-friendly online platform or mobile app for your tutoring marketplace, featuring tutor profiles, scheduling tools, lesson planning, video conferencing, interactive whiteboards, progress tracking, and payment processing capabilities, to facilitate seamless communication and collaboration between students and tutors.
- Offer a range of tutoring services and educational resources to students, including one-on-one tutoring sessions, group classes, homework help, exam preparation, study guides, practice tests, and learning materials, tailored to individual learning needs, academic goals, and learning objectives, to maximize student engagement and learning outcomes.
- Market and promote your online tutoring platform through digital marketing channels, social media campaigns, educational partnerships, student referrals, and parent networks, while leveraging testimonials, success stories, and student achievements to build

credibility, trust, and brand awareness in the online education market.

80. Invest in Cryptocurrencies with High Growth Potential:

Investing in cryptocurrencies with high growth potential involves purchasing digital assets or tokens issued on blockchain networks, such as Bitcoin, Ethereum, or other altcoins, with the expectation of long-term capital appreciation and investment returns due to market adoption, technological innovation, and demand for decentralized finance (DeFi) solutions.

Case Study:

Michael Thompson diversified his investment portfolio by allocating a portion of his capital to cryptocurrencies with high growth potential. By conducting research, analyzing market trends, and identifying promising projects and protocols, Michael invested in cryptocurrencies with strong fundamentals, innovative use cases, and supportive communities, earning significant returns as the cryptocurrency market grew and matured.

Getting Started:
- Educate yourself about cryptocurrencies, blockchain technology, and decentralized finance (DeFi), understanding the underlying principles, technologies, risks, and opportunities associated with investing in digital assets, and stay informed about market developments, regulatory changes, and industry trends.

- Research and analyze potential cryptocurrencies for investment, considering factors such as project team, technology roadmap, community engagement, market adoption, liquidity, security, and regulatory compliance, to identify promising projects with long-term growth potential and investment value.
- Diversify your cryptocurrency investment portfolio across different asset classes, such as major cryptocurrencies (e.g., Bitcoin, Ethereum), altcoins, DeFi tokens, non-fungible tokens (NFTs), or tokenized assets, spreading your risk exposure and maximizing potential returns in various market conditions.
- Develop an investment strategy and risk management plan for cryptocurrency investing, setting clear investment objectives, entry and exit criteria, asset allocation targets, and profit-taking strategies, while maintaining a disciplined approach to portfolio management, asset rebalancing, and performance monitoring.
- Monitor and track your cryptocurrency investments actively, using cryptocurrency exchanges, portfolio management tools, and market analytics platforms to evaluate performance, assess market trends, and adjust your investment strategy based on changing market dynamics, while staying vigilant against fraud, scams, and security threats in the cryptocurrency ecosystem.

81. **Start a Successful Virtual Assistant Staffing Agency:**

Starting a successful virtual assistant staffing agency involves recruiting, training, and matching virtual assistants with clients seeking administrative, clerical, or specialized support services remotely, providing flexible staffing solutions and outsourcing options for businesses and entrepreneurs.

Case Study:

Emily Johnson founded a virtual assistant staffing agency specializing in providing virtual administrative support to small businesses and startups. By building a network of skilled virtual assistants, offering personalized matching services, and providing ongoing training and support, Emily's agency became a trusted partner for clients seeking remote assistance, generating revenue through service fees and subscription plans.

Getting Started:

- Define your virtual assistant staffing agency's target market, client industries, and service offerings, identifying the specific administrative tasks, skills, and expertise required by clients, and tailoring your staffing solutions to meet their needs and preferences.
- Recruit and onboard virtual assistants with diverse skills, backgrounds, and experience levels, sourcing candidates through online job platforms, social media channels, freelance networks, and professional associations, and conducting thorough vetting, interviews, and assessments to ensure quality and reliability.
- Establish processes and systems for matching virtual assistants with clients, including client consultations, needs assessments, job postings, candidate screening, skill matching, contract negotiations, and onboarding

procedures, to facilitate successful client-virtual assistant engagements and long-term partnerships.
- Provide ongoing support, training, and supervision for virtual assistants, offering resources, tools, and professional development opportunities to enhance their skills, productivity, and job satisfaction, while fostering a collaborative and supportive virtual work environment conducive to remote teamwork and communication.
- Market and promote your virtual assistant staffing agency through digital marketing channels, networking events, industry forums, and client referrals, showcasing your agency's expertise, reliability, and value proposition in providing high-quality virtual assistant services tailored to clients' needs and business objectives.

82. Offer Specialized Insurance Consulting or Risk Management Services:

Offering specialized insurance consulting or risk management services involves providing advisory, analytical, and strategic support to businesses, organizations, and individuals in assessing, mitigating, and managing risks associated with insurance coverage, claims management, and regulatory compliance.

Case Study:

Daniel Smith established an insurance consulting firm specializing in risk assessment and insurance solutions for small businesses. By conducting risk audits, evaluating insurance policies, and advising clients on coverage options and risk mitigation strategies, Daniel's firm helped clients optimize their insurance portfolios, reduce exposure to liabilities, and navigate complex insurance regulations, generating revenue through consulting fees and insurance brokerage commissions.

Getting Started:

- Identify your insurance consulting niche, focus area, and service offerings within the insurance industry, such as risk assessment, insurance policy review, claims management, captive insurance, cyber risk, business continuity planning, or regulatory compliance, based on your expertise, market demand, and client needs.
- Build a team of insurance experts, risk analysts, actuaries, legal advisors, and compliance specialists with specialized knowledge and experience in insurance consulting, risk management, insurance law, and regulatory compliance, to deliver comprehensive and tailored solutions to clients.
- Conduct comprehensive risk assessments and insurance audits for clients, analyzing their business operations, assets, liabilities, and insurance coverage to identify gaps, exposures, and opportunities for risk reduction, insurance optimization, and cost savings, while ensuring alignment with industry standards and regulatory requirements.
- Develop customized insurance solutions and risk management strategies for clients, including insurance program design, coverage recommendations, policy negotiations, claims advocacy, loss prevention measures, and risk transfer mechanisms, to address specific risks, protect assets, and mitigate financial losses in the event of unforeseen events or liabilities.

- Provide ongoing support, monitoring, and review of insurance programs and risk management initiatives, staying abreast of market trends, emerging risks, and regulatory changes, while advising clients on insurance renewals, policy updates, claims handling, and risk mitigation strategies, to optimize insurance coverage and protect clients' interests in a dynamic business environment.

83. Develop and Sell a Successful Online Craft or DIY Marketplace:

Developing and selling a successful online craft or DIY marketplace involves creating a digital platform or website that connects crafters, makers, and artisans with buyers interested in handmade or unique products, providing a marketplace for buying, selling, and showcasing creative goods.

Case Study:

- Sarah Johnson launched an online craft marketplace featuring handmade jewelry, home decor, and artisanal goods. By curating a diverse selection of products, supporting independent artists, and promoting handmade craftsmanship, Sarah's marketplace attracted a loyal customer base, generated revenue through transaction fees, and provided a platform for artisans to showcase their talents and products.

- **Getting Started:**
- Define your online craft marketplace's niche, focus area, and target audience within the craft and DIY community, such as handmade jewelry, woodworking, sewing,

ceramics, or paper crafts, based on market trends, consumer demand, and your passion for creative arts and crafts.
- Build a network of crafters, makers, and artisans interested in selling their handmade or DIY products on your online marketplace, inviting artists to join your platform, create vendor profiles, list their products, and manage their inventory, while providing tools, resources, and support for sellers to succeed.
- Develop an intuitive and visually appealing online platform or mobile app for your craft marketplace, featuring product listings, seller profiles, search filters, customer reviews, secure payment processing, and shipping logistics, to facilitate seamless transactions and enhance the shopping experience for buyers.
- Implement marketing and promotion strategies to attract buyers to your online craft marketplace, including social media campaigns, email newsletters, influencer partnerships, craft fairs, and seasonal promotions, while fostering a sense of community, creativity, and collaboration among buyers and sellers on your platform.
- Monetize your online craft marketplace through various revenue streams, such as listing fees, transaction fees, membership subscriptions, premium features, sponsored listings, and affiliate partnerships, while reinvesting in platform development, seller support, and marketing initiatives to grow your marketplace and expand its reach in the craft and DIY market.

84. Invest in Blue-Chip Mutual Funds for Long-Term Growth:

Investing in blue-chip mutual funds for long-term growth involves allocating capital to mutual funds that invest in established, financially stable, and industry-leading companies with strong track records of growth, profitability, and dividend payments, to achieve capital appreciation and wealth accumulation over time.

Case Study:

David Brown invested in blue-chip mutual funds that tracked major stock market indices, such as the S&P 500 or Dow Jones Industrial Average (DJIA). By diversifying his investment portfolio across a range of blue-chip stocks in different sectors and industries, David benefited from broad market exposure, reduced risk, and competitive returns, while enjoying the convenience and professional management offered by mutual funds.

Getting Started:

- Research and select blue-chip mutual funds with a history of consistent performance, low expense ratios, experienced fund managers, and diversified portfolios of high-quality stocks from well-established companies, focusing on factors such as investment objectives, fund size, risk profile, and investment strategy.
- Determine your investment goals, time horizon, risk tolerance, and asset allocation preferences before investing in blue-chip mutual funds, considering factors such as retirement planning, wealth preservation, college savings, or long-term financial goals, and aligning your

investment strategy with your financial objectives and risk appetite.
- Invest in blue-chip mutual funds through various channels, including online brokerage platforms, financial advisors, investment firms, or employer-sponsored retirement plans, using lump-sum investments, periodic contributions, or systematic investment plans (SIPs) to build a diversified portfolio of mutual funds over time.
- Monitor and review your blue-chip mutual fund investments regularly, evaluating fund performance, portfolio composition, and market trends, while rebalancing your investment portfolio as needed to maintain alignment with your investment objectives, risk profile, and long-term financial goals.

85. Start a Successful Content Marketing Agency:

Starting a successful content marketing agency involves providing strategic content creation, distribution, and promotion services to businesses, brands, and organizations, helping them attract, engage, and convert their target audience through compelling and valuable content across various channels.

Case Study:

Rebecca Miller founded a content marketing agency specializing in blog writing, social media management, and email marketing campaigns. By collaborating with clients to develop content strategies, producing high-quality content, and analyzing performance metrics, Rebecca's agency helped clients increase brand awareness, drive website traffic, and generate leads, earning revenue through retainer contracts and project-based fees.

Getting Started:

- Define your content marketing agency's niche, focus area, and service offerings within the content marketing landscape, such as content strategy development, content creation, content distribution, social media management, email marketing, SEO content, or video production, based on your expertise, market demand, and client needs.
- Build a team of content creators, writers, editors, graphic designers, videographers, and marketing specialists with diverse skills and experience in content marketing, digital storytelling, brand messaging, and audience engagement, to deliver creative and impactful content solutions to clients.
- Develop customized content strategies and campaigns for clients, aligning content objectives with business goals, target audience needs, brand voice, and competitive positioning, while incorporating keyword research, audience segmentation, content calendars, and performance metrics to drive content effectiveness and ROI.
- Create high-quality and engaging content assets for clients, including blog posts, articles, whitepapers, infographics, videos, podcasts, case studies, social media posts, and email newsletters, tailored to specific platforms, formats, and distribution channels, to maximize audience reach, engagement, and conversion opportunities.

- Measure and analyze content performance, using analytics tools, KPIs, and metrics to track content engagement, website traffic, conversion rates, and ROI, while optimizing content strategies, distribution channels, and messaging based on data insights and feedback, to continuously improve content effectiveness and achieve client objectives.

86. **Offer Specialized Corporate Training or Development Programs:**

Offering specialized corporate training or development programs involves designing, delivering, and facilitating customized learning experiences, workshops, and skill-building initiatives for organizations, employees, and executives to enhance professional competencies, performance, and organizational effectiveness.

Case Study:

Jonathan Carter established a corporate training firm specializing in leadership development and team building workshops. By conducting needs assessments, designing tailored training programs, and delivering interactive and experiential learning experiences, Jonathan's firm helped companies improve employee engagement, morale, and productivity, generating revenue through training fees and consulting services.

Getting Started:

- Identify your corporate training niche, focus area, and service offerings within the corporate learning and development space, such as leadership training, team building, sales training, communication skills, diversity training, change management, or soft skills development, based on market demand, industry trends, and client needs.

- Build a team of training facilitators, instructional designers, subject matter experts, and organizational development specialists with expertise in adult learning principles, instructional design methodologies, training delivery techniques, and industry-specific knowledge, to develop and deliver impactful training programs for clients.
- Customize training programs and workshops for clients, conducting training needs assessments, identifying learning objectives, designing training materials, and developing engaging and interactive learning experiences using a variety of formats, methods, and technologies to address specific skill gaps, learning preferences, and organizational goals.
- Deliver training programs and workshops onsite or virtually, using interactive presentations, group activities, case studies, role-playing exercises, simulations, and feedback sessions to engage participants, foster collaboration, and facilitate skill acquisition, while providing ongoing support, coaching, and reinforcement to ensure learning transfer and behavior change.
- Evaluate training effectiveness and impact, collecting feedback from participants, supervisors, and stakeholders, measuring learning outcomes, behavior changes, and performance improvements, while iterating on training content, delivery methods, and program

structures based on evaluation results and client feedback to continuously enhance training quality and value.

87. Develop and Sell a Successful Online Gardening or Landscaping Platform:

Developing and selling a successful online gardening or landscaping platform involves creating a digital marketplace or platform that connects gardening enthusiasts, landscapers, and gardening service providers with customers seeking gardening advice, products, and services, offering a platform for buying, selling, and sharing gardening-related content and resources.

Case Study:

Jessica Lee launched an online gardening platform featuring gardening tips, tutorials, and product recommendations. By building a community of gardeners, sharing valuable content, and partnering with gardening brands, Jessica's platform attracted a loyal audience, generated revenue through affiliate marketing, sponsored content, and product sales, and provided a platform for gardeners to connect and share their passion for gardening.

Getting Started:

- Define your online gardening or landscaping platform's target audience, focus area, and value proposition, identifying the specific gardening topics, interests, and needs of your audience, and tailoring your platform's content, features, and offerings to meet their gardening goals and preferences.

- Build a network of gardening experts, landscapers, horticulturists, and gardening enthusiasts to contribute content, share insights, and engage with your platform's community, recruiting contributors through guest blogging, influencer partnerships, and user-generated content campaigns to enrich your platform's content and user experience.
- Develop an intuitive and user-friendly online platform or mobile app for your gardening community, featuring gardening articles, tutorials, videos, forums, product reviews, marketplace listings, and social networking tools, to facilitate knowledge sharing, inspiration, and collaboration among gardeners and landscaping professionals.
- Monetize your online gardening platform through various revenue streams, such as affiliate marketing, sponsored content, advertising, premium memberships, e-commerce sales, and subscription services, while maintaining transparency, authenticity, and trustworthiness in recommending products and services to your audience.
- Grow and nurture your gardening community through community engagement, content curation, social media promotion, email newsletters, and events, fostering a supportive and interactive environment where gardeners can connect, learn, and share their gardening experiences, while positioning your platform as a trusted resource and destination for gardening enthusiasts.

88. Invest in High-Quality Real Estate Crowdfunding Projects:

Investing in high-quality real estate crowdfunding projects involves pooling capital with other investors to fund real estate developments, acquisitions, or renovations through online crowdfunding platforms, offering opportunities to participate in real estate investments with lower capital requirements, diversification benefits, and potential returns.

Case Study:

Alex Johnson invested in a real estate crowdfunding platform that specialized in commercial properties and residential developments. By reviewing project details, analyzing financial projections, and assessing property fundamentals, Alex diversified his investment portfolio, earned passive income from rental yields and property appreciation, and enjoyed the benefits of real estate ownership without the responsibilities of property management.

Getting Started:

- Research and evaluate real estate crowdfunding platforms that offer investment opportunities in commercial, residential, or mixed-use properties, assessing platform reputation, investment offerings, due diligence processes, fees, and investor protections to select platforms that align with your investment goals and risk tolerance.
- Diversify your real estate crowdfunding investments across different property types, locations, and investment strategies, spreading your risk exposure and maximizing potential returns while mitigating risks associated with

individual properties or market segments, to achieve portfolio diversification and risk-adjusted returns.

- Review and analyze investment opportunities on real estate crowdfunding platforms, conducting due diligence on project sponsors, property valuations, market dynamics, financial projections, and investment terms, to make informed investment decisions based on risk-return profiles, investment objectives, and investment time horizons.

- Monitor and track the performance of your real estate crowdfunding investments, assessing property occupancy rates, rental income, property values, cash flows, and project milestones, while staying informed about market trends, regulatory changes, and economic indicators that may impact your investment portfolio and real estate holdings.

- Reinvest dividends and returns from real estate crowdfunding investments, diversifying your investment portfolio, compounding investment gains, and exploring new investment opportunities on crowdfunding platforms to grow your real estate portfolio and achieve long-term financial goals through passive real estate investing.

89. Start a Successful SEO (Search Engine Optimization) Agency:

Starting a successful SEO agency involves providing search engine optimization services to businesses, websites, and online platforms, helping them improve their visibility, ranking, and organic traffic on search engine results pages

(SERPs), to attract more visitors, leads, and customers through organic search.

Case Study:

Michael Adams founded an SEO agency specializing in on-page optimization, link building, and content marketing strategies. By implementing SEO best practices, conducting website audits, and optimizing clients' websites for relevant keywords and search intent, Michael's agency helped clients achieve higher search rankings, increased organic traffic, and improved online visibility, generating revenue through retainer contracts and performance-based fees.

Getting Started:

- Define your SEO agency's niche, focus area, and service offerings within the SEO industry, such as technical SEO, content optimization, local SEO, e-commerce SEO, or enterprise SEO, based on your expertise, market demand, and client needs, and differentiate your agency by offering specialized services or industry expertise.
- Build a team of SEO experts, digital marketers, content creators, web developers, and data analysts with specialized skills and experience in search engine optimization, keyword research, competitor analysis, link building, content strategy, and analytics, to deliver comprehensive and results-driven SEO solutions to clients.
- Develop customized SEO strategies and campaigns for clients, conducting website audits, keyword research, and competitor analysis to identify optimization opportunities, technical issues, and content gaps, and devising tailored SEO plans and recommendations to

improve website performance, user experience, and search visibility.

- Implement SEO tactics and best practices on clients' websites, optimizing website structure, meta tags, headings, content, images, URLs, and internal links to align with search engine algorithms and user intent, while monitoring performance metrics, tracking keyword rankings, and analyzing traffic data to measure SEO effectiveness and identify areas for improvement.

- Provide ongoing SEO monitoring, optimization, and reporting services to clients, conducting regular performance reviews, analyzing SEO trends, and adapting strategies based on algorithm updates, market changes, and client feedback, to ensure sustained organic growth, competitive rankings, and maximum ROI for clients' SEO investments.

90. Offer Specialized Sustainability Consulting or Green Energy Solutions:

Offering specialized sustainability consulting or green energy solutions involves providing advisory, technical, and strategic support to businesses, organizations, and governments in implementing environmentally sustainable practices, renewable energy solutions, and green technologies to reduce carbon footprint, conserve resources, and promote sustainability.

Case Study:

Laura Anderson established a sustainability consulting firm specializing in energy efficiency audits and renewable energy projects. By conducting sustainability assessments, identifying energy-saving opportunities, and recommending green initiatives, Laura's firm helped clients reduce energy costs, enhance environmental performance, and achieve sustainability goals, generating revenue through consulting fees, project implementation, and government grants.

Getting Started:

- Identify your sustainability consulting niche, focus area, and service offerings within the sustainability and green energy sector, such as energy management, carbon footprint reduction, renewable energy adoption, green building certification, or sustainable supply chain management, based on your expertise, market demand, and client needs.
- Build a team of sustainability experts, environmental engineers, energy auditors, and green technology specialists with specialized knowledge and experience in sustainability consulting, energy management, renewable energy systems, carbon accounting, and environmental regulations, to deliver customized solutions and actionable recommendations to clients.
- Conduct sustainability assessments and energy audits for clients, analyzing energy consumption, waste generation, greenhouse gas emissions, and environmental impacts across their operations, facilities, and supply chain, to identify cost-effective measures, technology upgrades, and behavior changes that can improve resource efficiency and reduce environmental footprint.
- Develop tailored sustainability plans and green energy strategies for clients, setting measurable goals, targets, and performance indicators, and recommending

- initiatives such as energy-efficient retrofits, renewable energy installations, waste reduction programs, water conservation measures, and sustainability certifications, to drive continuous improvement and progress towards sustainability objectives.
- Provide ongoing support, monitoring, and verification services to clients, tracking progress against sustainability goals, benchmarking performance metrics, and reporting outcomes to stakeholders, while advocating for policy changes, industry standards, and community engagement initiatives to advance sustainability practices and create positive environmental impact.

91. Start a Successful Software Development Outsourcing Company:

Starting a successful software development outsourcing company involves offering customized software development services to businesses, startups, and enterprises, leveraging a team of skilled software engineers, developers, and IT professionals to deliver high-quality software solutions tailored to client requirements.

Case Study:

Emily Adams founded a software development outsourcing company specializing in web and mobile app development. By assembling a team of experienced developers, adopting agile development methodologies, and maintaining open communication with clients, Emily's company delivered innovative software solutions, earned positive client testimonials, and expanded its client base through referrals and word-of-mouth marketing.

Getting Started:

- Identify your software development niche, focus area, and target market within the technology industry, such as web development, mobile app development, enterprise software solutions, SaaS products, e-commerce platforms, or IoT applications, based on market demand, industry trends, and your team's expertise.
- Build a team of talented software engineers, developers, designers, project managers, and quality assurance specialists with diverse skills and experience in software development, programming languages, frameworks, and technologies, to handle client projects, meet project deadlines, and deliver exceptional software solutions.
- Define your service offerings, pricing models, and engagement strategies for software development projects, including project-based pricing, hourly rates, retainer agreements, or milestone-based payments, while emphasizing transparency, flexibility, and value for clients to attract and retain customers.
- Develop a robust project management process, communication protocols, and quality assurance standards for software development projects, using collaboration tools, version control systems, project management software, and testing frameworks to streamline project workflows, ensure code quality, and meet client expectations.
- Market and promote your software development outsourcing company through digital marketing channels, professional networks, industry events, and

strategic partnerships, showcasing your team's expertise, past projects, client testimonials, and success stories to attract clients, build credibility, and grow your business in the competitive software outsourcing market.

92. Offer Specialized Diversity and Inclusion Consulting Services:

Offering specialized diversity and inclusion consulting services involves providing advisory, training, and coaching services to organizations, HR departments, and leadership teams, helping them foster inclusive workplaces, cultivate diverse talent, and promote equity and belonging within their organizations.

Case Study:

Marcus Harris established a diversity and inclusion consulting firm focusing on diversity training, cultural competency workshops, and equity assessments. By partnering with corporate clients, conducting diversity audits, and implementing inclusive practices, Marcus's firm helped organizations improve workplace diversity, reduce bias, and enhance employee engagement and retention, generating revenue through consulting contracts and customized training programs.

Getting Started:

- Identify your expertise, niche, and focus area within the diversity and inclusion field, such as unconscious bias training, inclusive leadership development, cultural competency workshops, diversity recruiting, or employee

resource group facilitation, based on your background, qualifications, and market demand.
- Build a network of diversity and inclusion experts, trainers, facilitators, and subject matter specialists with expertise in areas such as diversity management, organizational psychology, cultural anthropology, social justice, and human resources, to collaborate on consulting projects, deliver training programs, and provide thought leadership.
- Develop customized diversity and inclusion solutions for clients, conducting organizational assessments, diversity audits, and climate surveys to identify areas for improvement, developing diversity strategies, action plans, and policies tailored to each client's needs, culture, and goals, while fostering a culture of inclusion and belonging.
- Deliver impactful diversity and inclusion training programs, workshops, and seminars for employees, managers, and executives, using interactive exercises, case studies, role-playing scenarios, and facilitated discussions to raise awareness, build empathy, and promote allyship, while providing ongoing support and guidance to organizations on their diversity journey.
- Measure and evaluate the effectiveness of diversity and inclusion initiatives, tracking key performance indicators, diversity metrics, and employee feedback to assess progress, identify areas for improvement, and demonstrate ROI to clients, while advocating for continuous learning, evolution, and innovation in diversity and inclusion practices.

93. Develop and Sell a Successful Online Mindfulness or Meditation Platform:

Developing and selling a successful online mindfulness or meditation platform involves creating a digital platform or app that offers guided meditation sessions, mindfulness exercises, relaxation techniques, and mental wellness resources to users seeking stress relief, relaxation, and personal growth.

Case Study:

Sarah Thompson founded an online mindfulness platform featuring guided meditation sessions, stress management courses, and mindfulness tools. By partnering with meditation teachers, mental health experts, and wellness coaches, Sarah's platform attracted a global audience, generated revenue through subscription plans and premium content, and provided users with accessible and effective mindfulness resources.

Getting Started:

- Define your target audience and user demographics within the mindfulness and wellness market, such as beginners, experienced meditators, corporate professionals, students, or specific interest groups, based on market research, user surveys, and audience segmentation, to tailor your platform's content and features to their needs.
- Curate a library of guided meditation sessions, mindfulness exercises, breathing techniques, and relaxation practices from experienced meditation teachers, mental health professionals, and wellness

experts, ensuring diversity, accessibility, and relevance to users' preferences, goals, and skill levels.

- Develop an intuitive and user-friendly online platform or mobile app for delivering mindfulness content and resources, incorporating features such as personalized recommendations, progress tracking, meditation timers, mood tracking, and community forums to enhance user engagement, retention, and satisfaction.

- Monetize your online mindfulness platform through subscription-based models, freemium plans, one-time purchases, in-app purchases, or donation-based support, offering users a range of pricing options, membership tiers, and value-added benefits to access premium content, features, and exclusive perks.

- Promote and market your mindfulness platform through digital marketing channels, social media platforms, wellness forums, and partnerships with influencers, therapists, and health organizations, emphasizing the benefits of mindfulness, stress reduction, and mental wellness to attract users, drive engagement, and grow your platform's user base.

94. Invest in High-Quality Art Funds or Collectibles Portfolios:

Investing in high-quality art funds or collectibles portfolios involves allocating capital to investment vehicles, funds, or portfolios that specialize in acquiring, managing, and trading valuable artworks, rare collectibles, and cultural assets, offering potential returns through capital appreciation, diversification, and alternative investments.

Case Study:

David Martinez invested in an art fund that focused on contemporary art and emerging artists. By leveraging the expertise of art curators, collectors, and investment professionals, David gained exposure to the art market, diversified his investment portfolio, and enjoyed potential returns from art appreciation and art market trends, while benefiting from professional management and risk mitigation strategies.

Getting Started:

- Research and evaluate art funds, investment trusts, and collectibles portfolios offered by reputable financial institutions, asset managers, and investment firms specializing in art and collectibles, assessing factors such as fund track record, investment strategy, portfolio holdings, management fees, and liquidity terms to select suitable investment options.
- Determine your investment objectives, risk tolerance, and time horizon for investing in art funds or collectibles portfolios, considering factors such as portfolio diversification, asset allocation, liquidity needs, and long-term wealth preservation goals, to align your investment strategy with your financial circumstances and investment preferences.
- Understand the art market dynamics, trends, and valuation methodologies used in assessing artworks and collectibles, consulting art experts, auction houses, galleries, and art market reports to stay informed about market trends, artist performances, and investment

- opportunities in the art market, while conducting due diligence on potential investments.
- Monitor and review the performance of your art fund investments or collectibles portfolios regularly, tracking art market indices, portfolio valuations, auction results, and fund performance metrics, while staying updated on regulatory changes, tax implications, and market developments affecting art investments, to make informed decisions and adjustments to your investment portfolio.
- Diversify your investment portfolio across different asset classes, including equities, fixed income, real estate, and alternative investments such as art funds or collectibles portfolios, to mitigate risks, enhance returns, and achieve portfolio balance and stability, while seeking professional advice and guidance from financial advisors or wealth managers specialized in art investments and wealth preservation strategies.

95. Develop and Sell a Successful Online Parenting or Childcare Platform:

Developing and selling a successful online parenting or childcare platform involves creating a digital platform or app that provides parents with resources, advice, tools, and community support for navigating various aspects of parenthood, child development, and family well-being, addressing parenting challenges and offering solutions for raising happy and healthy children.

Case Study:

Julia Rodriguez launched an online parenting platform featuring articles, videos, expert advice, and interactive forums for parents. By covering topics such as pregnancy, newborn care, toddler behavior, and parenting tips, Julia's platform attracted a large audience of parents seeking reliable information and support, monetizing through advertising, sponsored content, and premium memberships, while building a vibrant online community of engaged users.

Getting Started:

- Identify the target audience and key demographics within the parenting and childcare market, such as new parents, expectant mothers, working parents, or families with young children, based on market research, user surveys, and audience segmentation, to tailor your platform's content and features to their needs and preferences.
- Create valuable and informative content for your online parenting platform, including articles, blog posts, videos, podcasts, webinars, and downloadable resources, covering topics such as pregnancy, childbirth, breastfeeding, child nutrition, sleep training, positive discipline, and family activities, to provide parents with practical advice, expert insights, and actionable tips.
- Develop interactive features and community-building tools for your parenting platform, such as discussion forums, Q&A sessions, support groups, virtual events, and peer-to-peer networking, to foster engagement, collaboration, and connection among parents, while facilitating knowledge sharing, peer support, and social interaction within the parenting community.
- Monetize your online parenting platform through various revenue streams, such as display advertising, sponsored

content, affiliate marketing, premium memberships, e-commerce sales, and online courses or workshops, offering value-added services, exclusive content, and premium features to subscribers or paid members, while maintaining transparency, credibility, and trust with your audience.

- Promote and market your parenting platform through digital marketing channels, social media platforms, parenting forums, mommy groups, and partnerships with influencers, pediatricians, childcare experts, and family-oriented brands, leveraging user-generated content, testimonials, and word-of-mouth referrals to attract new users, drive traffic, and grow your platform's audience and community.

96. Investing in Yourself through Continuous Learning and Personal Development:

Investing in yourself through continuous learning and personal development involves dedicating time, resources, and effort to acquire new knowledge, skills, and experiences, enhance your expertise, and expand your capabilities in your chosen field or area of interest, to increase your earning potential, advance your career, and achieve your personal and professional goals.

Case Study:

David Johnson invested in his personal development by enrolling in online courses, attending workshops, and pursuing certifications related to his career in digital marketing. By upgrading his skills in areas such as search engine optimization

(SEO), content marketing, and social media advertising, David improved his job performance, increased his earning potential, and unlocked new opportunities for career advancement and professional growth.

Getting Started:

- Assess your strengths, weaknesses, interests, and career goals to identify areas for improvement and development, reflecting on your skills, experiences, passions, and aspirations, and evaluating the knowledge gaps, skills gaps, or professional challenges you want to address through continuous learning and personal development.
- Set clear and achievable learning objectives, goals, and milestones for your personal development journey, establishing SMART (Specific, Measurable, Achievable, Relevant, Time-bound) goals, action plans, and accountability mechanisms to track your progress, measure your success, and stay motivated and focused on your learning goals.
- Explore various learning opportunities and resources available to you, such as online courses, webinars, workshops, conferences, seminars, books, podcasts, mentorship programs, or professional networks, seeking out high-quality, reputable sources of education and training that align with your learning preferences, learning style, and career objectives.
- Invest time, effort, and resources into your continuous learning and personal development activities, prioritizing self-directed learning, self-discipline, and self-motivation to stay engaged, disciplined, and committed to your learning goals, while maintaining a growth mindset,

resilience, and adaptability in the face of challenges and setbacks.
- Apply and integrate your new knowledge, skills, and insights into your daily work, projects, and activities, actively seeking opportunities to practice, experiment, and apply what you've learned, while seeking feedback, mentorship, and support from peers, colleagues, or industry experts to accelerate your learning curve and maximize your personal and professional development outcomes.

97. Become a Professional Athlete:

Becoming a professional athlete involves dedicating years of training, practice, and competition to excel in a specific sport, showcasing exceptional talent, athleticism, and performance to attract the attention of scouts, coaches, and sports agents, and ultimately securing contracts or endorsements with professional sports teams, leagues, or sponsors.

Case Study:

LeBron James pursued his dream of becoming a professional basketball player from a young age, honing his skills on the court and dominating high school basketball competitions. His exceptional talent and athleticism garnered widespread attention, making him one of the most highly touted prospects in basketball history. After forgoing college, LeBron entered the NBA Draft in 2003 and was selected as the first overall pick by the Cleveland Cavaliers. Since then, LeBron has enjoyed a legendary career, earning numerous accolades, MVP awards, and championships while solidifying his status as one of the greatest basketball players of all time.

Getting Started:

- Choose a sport or athletic discipline that aligns with your interests, talents, and physical abilities, considering factors such as your natural athleticism, competitive drive, and long-term career aspirations, to focus your training and development efforts on a sport where you have the greatest potential for success and fulfillment.
- Establish a structured training regimen, workout routine, and practice schedule tailored to your sport-specific goals, training needs, and performance objectives, incorporating elements such as strength training, conditioning, skill development, and game strategy to enhance your athletic performance, agility, and endurance.
- Compete in local, regional, and national-level competitions, tournaments, and events within your sport, gaining valuable experience, exposure, and recognition among coaches, scouts, and talent evaluators, while showcasing your skills, athleticism, and competitive spirit in front of audiences and potential sponsors.
- Seek guidance, mentorship, and coaching from experienced athletes, trainers, and coaches who can provide expert advice, technical instruction, and psychological support to help you overcome challenges, refine your technique, and maximize your potential as an athlete, while staying motivated, disciplined, and resilient throughout your journey.
- Pursue opportunities to advance your career and achieve professional status in your sport, such as joining elite

training programs, participating in talent development camps, attending sports combines or tryouts, or seeking representation from sports agents or agencies specializing in athlete management and career development, to position yourself for success in the competitive world of professional sports.

98. Start a Successful Social Media Management Agency:

Starting a successful social media management agency involves leveraging your expertise in digital marketing, content creation, and social media strategy to help businesses and brands enhance their online presence, engage with their target audience, and achieve their marketing objectives through effective social media marketing campaigns and initiatives.

Case Study:

Emily Thompson founded a social media management agency specializing in helping small businesses and startups elevate their social media presence. By offering comprehensive services such as content creation, community management, advertising, and analytics, Emily's agency successfully grew its client base and reputation in the industry. Through strategic planning, creative campaigns, and data-driven insights, Emily's team delivered tangible results for clients, including increased brand awareness, customer engagement, and sales conversions, establishing her agency as a trusted partner for businesses seeking to succeed in the digital landscape.

Getting Started:

- Define your agency's niche, target market, and unique value proposition within the social media management industry, identifying areas of specialization, industry verticals, or client demographics that align with your expertise, interests, and market opportunities, to differentiate your agency and attract ideal clients.
- Develop a range of social media management services and packages tailored to the needs, goals, and budgets of your target clients, including content creation, posting schedules, community engagement, influencer partnerships, advertising campaigns, and performance analytics, offering scalable solutions and customizable options to meet diverse client requirements.
- Build a strong online presence and professional brand identity for your social media management agency, creating a visually appealing website, portfolio, and social media profiles to showcase your expertise, previous work, client testimonials, and success stories, while optimizing your online visibility, search rankings, and credibility to attract potential clients and inquiries.
- Cultivate strategic partnerships and collaborations with complementary service providers, industry influencers, and business networks to expand your agency's reach, referral network, and client pipeline, while attending industry events, conferences, and networking gatherings to connect with potential clients, collaborators, and industry peers.

- Deliver exceptional value, results, and customer service to your clients, exceeding their expectations, addressing their needs, and building long-term relationships and loyalty, while continuously refining your service offerings, processes, and strategies based on client feedback, industry trends, and emerging technologies to stay competitive and innovative in the dynamic field of social media management.

99. Offer Specialized Legal Consulting or Compliance Services:

Offering specialized legal consulting or compliance services involves providing expert advice, guidance, and support to businesses, organizations, and individuals on complex legal matters, regulatory requirements, and compliance issues, helping them navigate legal challenges, mitigate risks, and ensure regulatory compliance in their operations and business activities.

Case Study:

Michael Johnson established a boutique legal consulting firm specializing in regulatory compliance for healthcare organizations. Leveraging his background in healthcare law and regulatory affairs, Michael's firm provided comprehensive compliance solutions, risk assessments, policy development, and training programs to healthcare providers, ensuring compliance with HIPAA, FDA regulations, and other industry standards. By offering tailored solutions and personalized service, Michael's firm earned a reputation for excellence and became a trusted advisor to healthcare clients nationwide.

Getting Started:

- Identify a niche or area of specialization within the legal consulting or compliance field based on your expertise, experience, and market demand, focusing on industries, sectors, or regulatory areas where there is a need for specialized legal advice, compliance support, or risk management solutions.
- Establish your legal consulting firm's value proposition, service offerings, and competitive advantage, articulating the unique benefits, expertise, and value that your firm brings to clients, such as industry knowledge, regulatory expertise, personalized service, or innovative solutions, to differentiate your firm and attract clients.
- Develop a network of industry contacts, referral sources, and strategic alliances within your target market, including industry associations, professional networks, legal communities, and business forums, to generate leads, referrals, and opportunities for collaboration and partnership with potential clients, collaborators, and industry peers.
- Invest in professional development, ongoing education, and certifications relevant to your specialized area of legal consulting or compliance services, staying informed about changes in laws, regulations, and industry standards, while continuously upgrading your skills, knowledge, and expertise to provide value-added insights and solutions to your clients.
- Provide high-quality, responsive, and personalized service to your clients, delivering practical, actionable

advice, solutions, and recommendations tailored to their specific needs, challenges, and objectives, while building trust, credibility, and long-term relationships with clients through transparency, integrity, and professionalism in your legal consulting practice.

100. Become a High-Profile Musician:

Becoming a high-profile musician involves honing your musical talent, building a unique brand and persona, and navigating the music industry to achieve success, recognition, and longevity in your music career. From mastering your craft and cultivating a loyal fan base to securing record deals, releasing hit songs, and performing sold-out concerts, aspiring musicians must combine creativity, perseverance, and strategic planning to rise to the top of the music industry.

Case Study:

Aubrey Drake Graham, known professionally as Drake, rose to prominence as a high-profile musician through his exceptional talent, versatility, and entrepreneurial spirit. From his early days as an actor on the television series "Degrassi: The Next Generation" to his transition into music as a rapper, singer, and songwriter, Drake captivated audiences with his distinctive style, introspective lyrics, and catchy melodies. By leveraging social media platforms, collaborating with established artists, and releasing a series of successful mixtapes and albums, Drake built a massive following and became one of the best-selling artists of all time. His strategic partnerships with record labels, endorsements, and business ventures further solidified his status as a global music icon, demonstrating how ambition, innovation, and perseverance can propel a musician to high-profile success in the competitive music industry.

Getting Started:

- Develop your musical talent, skills, and creativity through dedicated practice, training, and experimentation, mastering your instrument, voice, or production techniques to create original and compelling music that resonates with audiences and distinguishes you from other musicians in the industry.
- Build your brand and persona as a musician, crafting a distinct image, style, and identity that reflects your personality, values, and artistic vision, while engaging with fans, influencers, and media outlets through social media, live performances, interviews, and other promotional channels to cultivate a loyal and engaged fan base.
- Navigate the music industry landscape by networking with industry professionals, attending music conferences, showcases, and festivals, and seeking advice and mentorship from experienced artists, managers, and industry insiders, to gain insights into the business side of the music industry and identify opportunities for growth and exposure.
- Create and release high-quality music consistently, whether through singles, EPs, or albums, showcasing your talent, versatility, and creativity across different genres, while leveraging digital distribution platforms, streaming services, and social media marketing to reach a wider audience and generate buzz around your music releases.

- Pursue opportunities to perform live, collaborate with other artists, and secure record deals, publishing contracts, or licensing agreements to monetize your music, expand your reach, and build your reputation as a high-profile musician, while staying true to your artistic vision, integrity, and passion for music throughout your career journey.

Bonus: Innovate an Out-of-the-Box Idea:

Innovating an out-of-the-box idea involves thinking creatively, challenging conventional wisdom, and identifying unconventional solutions to address a problem or capitalize on an opportunity in a novel and innovative way. By pushing the boundaries of imagination, embracing risk-taking, and daring to pursue unconventional paths, individuals and entrepreneurs can unlock new possibilities, disrupt industries, and create significant value and impact.

Case Study:

Gary Dahl, an advertising copywriter, famously generated $15 million in revenue by selling rocks he sourced from a Mexican beach as pets for $4 each. In 1975, Dahl introduced the concept of the "Pet Rock," a simple yet absurd idea that captured the imagination of millions of Americans. Packaged in a cardboard box with air holes and a tongue-in-cheek instruction manual, the Pet Rock became a cultural phenomenon, offering consumers a humorous and low-maintenance alternative to traditional pets. Despite its seemingly ridiculous premise, the Pet Rock craze swept the nation, with Dahl's innovative marketing and clever packaging turning an ordinary rock into a must-have novelty item and a symbol of 1970s pop culture. The success of the Pet Rock serves as a testament to the power of creativity, humor, and novelty in capturing consumer interest and driving sales, showcasing how an out-of-the-box idea can lead to extraordinary success.

www.ingramcontent.com/pod-product-compliance
Lightning Source LLC
Chambersburg PA
CBHW052203220526
45471CB00004B/1798